LIVING THAT LIFE
SHADOWS OF THE PAST

Written By:
Demetrius Collins

Published by

Brookscraft Publishing
A Division of Brooks Craft LLC
Info@brookscraftpublishing.com
www.brookscraftpublishing.com

Author's Contact

To book the author as a speaker at your next event or to order bulk copies of this book, please, use the email below:

perfectedimageentertainment@gmail.com

Dedication

To my family, the foundation of my strength and inspiration:

To my wife, Sherry Collins, whose patience and unwavering support have been my guiding light through the long nights and distant days of writing. Your belief in me never wavered, even when the words seemed lost.

To my mother, Helen Collins, who instilled in me the value of perseverance and the love for words. Your lessons with that ruler in hand shaped not just my writing, but my character.

To my sister, Linda Walker, whose encouragement lifted me from the depths of discouragement and pushed me to embrace my creativity.

To my father, T.C. Collins Jr., whose unique way of motivating me taught me resilience and the courage to face life's challenges head-on. Your lessons in strength and skill have been my silent teachers.

To my brothers, Byron and Travis Collins, whose lives have been a testament to dedication and fatherhood. Watching you has shown me the profound impact of guidance and love.

And to my granddaughter, Allisa Rougely, whose memory is a poignant reminder of the fragility and preciousness of life. This story, filled with trials and triumphs, is a reflection of the resilience and unity that defines our family.

To every reader who finds a piece of their story within these pages, may you discover the life you are meant to live.

With love and gratitude, Demetrius Collins

About the Author

My name is Demetrius Collins. Many know me by the name of DT Collins. I am a 53 years old musician that loves playing the organ and piano at church. I also love singing and working with audio and video recording. I am an entrepreneur through my company called Perfect'd Image Publishing and Business Center. I write eBooks and this is my first novel. I am a videographer, photographer, graphic designer, content creator and an a.i. avatar designer. I love desinging and creating things from scratch whether it's a virtual avatar, poster, flyer, book, screenplay, recording music or writing a song. I love showing others how to do things that may come easy to me but challenging to someone else.

Demetrius Collins

Table Of Content

LIVING THAT LIFE

Chapter 1:

From Childhood Friends to Partners in Crime

In the heart of Temple, Texas, a tale of greed, desperation, and the consequences of criminal behavior unfold. This story is not for the faint of heart, as it delves into the lives of individuals who were driven by the allure of quick money and found themselves entangled in a web of crime and deception. The narrative follows two distinct groups of friends, once united but now divided by the choices they make and the paths they take.

Tyrone Turner was feared by others, who was a notorious criminal whose reputation preceded him. His life was a testament to the harsh realities of the streets, where survival often meant embracing a life of crime. Born into poverty and surrounded by violence, Tyrone learned early on that the world was a cruel and unforgiving place. With few options available to him, he turned to a life of crime to make ends meet and thus began his rise to infamy.

Leroy Mathis and Tyrone Turner were childhood friends who grew up in the same neighborhood. Leroy had started going to church during his later years, but he would let peer pressure get the best of him, even after he had gotten married. Their bond was forged in the fires of adversity, as they both came from difficult family backgrounds and found a sense of comfort in each other's company. As they grew older, their friendship evolved into a partnership in crime. What started as petty thefts and minor offenses escalated into more serious crimes, as they saw it as a way to escape their troubled lives and make quick cash.

LIVING THAT LIFE

Chapter 2:

The Young Life

On a cool autumn night, Tyrone Turner and Leroy Mathis found themselves at a local bar, discussing their financial troubles with their friends Glenn Williams and Marcus. As the drinks flowed, so did the ideas for making quick cash. Glenn suggested breaking into a nearby mansion owned by a wealthy business owner who was going out of town. Despite first reservations, Tyrone and Leroy agreed to the plan, recruiting Marcus to help them carry it out.

The group spent days planning the break-in, carefully studying the layout of the house, and devising a strategy to avoid detection. Tyrone suggested that they do two jobs on the same night, with Leroy and his crew managing one while Tyrone took care of the other. The plan was risky, but the allure of a big payoff was too tempting to resist.

LIVING THAT LIFE

Chapter 3:

The Police Stakeout

Meanwhile, across town, Captain Allen Swinson made it clear that bringing down Tyrone was a top priority. Swinson was a seasoned officer with a reputation for getting results. He had assembled a SWAT team, equipped with the latest tactical gear, and they were ready to move at a moment's notice.

Officer Gerald Tisdale sat in his unmarked car, his eyes scanning the neighborhood. He had received an anonymous tip about a potential break-in, and his instincts told him that Tyrone Turner was involved. Tisdale had been tracking Tyrone for months, and tonight, he hoped to finally catch him in the act. Tisdale called for backup and requested SWAT to be a part of this raid.

LIVING THAT LIFE

Chapter 4:

The House Break-In

As they approached the house, Glenn's palms were slick with sweat. He tried to calm himself down, but the fear just kept building. He knew that once they went through with this, there was no turning back. The consequences could be severe, and he didn't know if he was ready to face them.

They had been surveilling this house for weeks. They knew the owners were out of town and that the place was ripe for the picking. They waited until the dead of night to make their move, slipping through an unlocked window in the back.

The plan was to split up and search for anything of value. Glenn's heart was pounding as he followed Leroy and Marcus towards the house. He couldn't shake the feeling that something was going to go wrong. What if they had gotten caught? What if someone was home? The thought of getting caught filled him with dread.

Once inside, they split up and began searching for anything of value. Leroy headed straight for the bedroom, while Glenn checked out the living room. Marcus made his way to the kitchen, hoping to find something of value.

As Leroy quietly made his way to the bedroom, he couldn't help but feel the adrenaline pumping through his veins. He had done this before, but never with so much on the line. Leroy saw a pair of pants with a wallet in it. He then realized that the house was not vacant. Leroy carefully reached for the wallet on the nightstand and felt a wave of relief wash over him as it came easily into his grasp. He noticed the bathroom light was on just as he was about to go through the dresser drawers, he started hearing noises. Before making his escape, suddenly another noise from the hallway sounded out loud causing his heart to start pounding as he listened intently. Leroy then entered the Livingroom just as he heard the bathroom door began to open and heard a loud voice saying who's in here, where's my gun? Leroy began running as he signaled for Glenn and Marcus to take off out the front door. But Leroy remembered the car was parked toward the back of the house.

Chapter 5:

The Escape

As they fled the scene, Glenn ran towards the car, while Leroy followed behind Marcus trying to run for the car, but chaos erupted around them causing them to take a different route. The sound of sirens blared in the distance as they panicked while sprinting through the dark streets running further away from the car. Marcus yelled out to Leroy, "that fool must've called the cops while he was in the bathroom". Leroy agreed as anger began to set in. They could hear the pounding of their own hearts as they tried to outrun the law.

As they found a hiding spot, Leroy's anger boiled over as he confronted Marcus. He couldn't believe they had come so close to getting caught. He was furious that they had not followed the plan. "Dude, what were you two idiots thinking?" he yelled. "We had everything planned out, and you two screwed it up!" Marcus looked at Leroy in shame and denial concerning what he was yelling about. Leroy continued saying, "This is all your fault," he said. "I thought that noise from the hall came from the man that lived there, but he was in the bathroom. But Marcus, it was you! If it wasn't for you, we wouldn't be in this mess."

Glenn sat in the car waiting for Leroy and Marcus to come on. Just as Glenn thought about driving off, he heard a short chirp from a police siren close by. Suddenly, the flashing lights illuminated the area, casting an eerie glow on the area where Leroy and

Marcus had run towards. Glenn thought, "hopefully they got away".

Meanwhile, across town as Tyrone and Wesley crept through the darkened rooms of the second house, the floorboards creaked beneath their feet, sending shivers down their spines. Every sound seemed magnified, and they held their breath, waiting for any sign of danger. The plan was risky, but they were willing to take the chance for the promise of a big payoff.

As Glenn waited for Leroy and Marcus inside of the get a way car, he began to get more worried, he thought, "should I leave or wait it out"? Panic set in as Glenn realized that his boys were trapped. Leroy said, "Run!" Marcus took off running, but was caught at once, while Leroy also tried but was tackled to the ground. Glenn, however, managed to stay unnoticed as he stayed hidden in the getaway car ducked down hoping to avoid the cops running by. After he thought it was safe, he looked up, saw nothing then cranked up and escaped the scene.

LIVING THAT LIFE

Chapter 6:

Tyrone's Escape

As the loud noise continued and now bright lights appeared, the back door of Glenn's car opens with a soft gentle voice saying, "Hey Glenn"? Glenn startled, glancing backward saying, "Tyrone". Tyrone begins saying, "Somebody tipped off the cops. Was it you? I think it was you! Why else would you be this close to our break-in"? You know what, never mind, just drive me out of here. "But Tyrone", Glenn replied. I live here. Tyrone said, "What? You live in this nice area, we should've hit up your place instead, Glenn nervously giggling saying, "this is my family home, I grew up here. Tyrone said, "It's okay, Calm down, I was just joking.

Come on, give me a ride home. It was a long quiet ride, then Tyrone said, look dude, I know where you live now. So, it's best not to say anything. Tyrone got out of the car and started walking towards his house. Glenn vowed to say nothing. That's good, Tyrone said as he gave a half smirk.

LIVING THAT LIFE

Chapter 7:

The Arrest

The aftermath of the break-in was devastating for all involved. Leroy and Marcus were arrested and charged with burglary and theft. They faced serious legal consequences, including fines and potential jail time. The impact on their relationships was equally severe.

As far as Tyrone is concerned, his arrest was the result of a meticulous investigation by the local police department. After weeks of surveillance and gathering evidence, they were finally able to make their move and apprehend Turner at his home.

LIVING THAT LIFE

Chapter 8:

The Trial of Marcus and Leroy

Marcus and Leroy trial was considered fair, but an event that could have been avoided if the thought of burglary had never been a thought in the first place. But with the community's support along with family, the judge had compassion for them because he knew their families. They were sentenced to only 3 years of prison with 10 years of probation.

But Marcus always had something to prove and could not keep his mouth shut and always ended up in fights. Fortunately, Leroy had fighting skills and had to help Marcus each time he would mouth off to inmates who were always bigger than he was. Leroy won but Marcus would get knocked out sometimes causing them to lose. Although they were only given 3 years of time to serve, another judge ended up taking over their cases due to favoritism. The new judge took over and kept adding time for every incident that happened. Leroy ended up with 10 years total with Marcus getting out within 9 in half a year.

LIVING THAT LIFE

Chapter 9:

The Trial of Tyrone

On the other hand, the trial of Tyrone Turner was a highly publicized event. The prosecution presented a strong case, detailing Tyrone's involvement in the robberies and his earlier criminal history. Witnesses, including Tyrone's former associates who had turned state's evidence, testified against him. The evidence seized from his house was presented, further strengthening the prosecution's case.

Tyrone's defense attorney tried to argue that the evidence was obtained illegally due to a technicality in the search warrant. However, the judge ruled that the evidence was admissible, dealing a significant blow to Tyrone's defense.

Throughout the trial, Tyrone kept a stoic expression, but his eyes betrayed a mix of anger and fear. He knew that the odds were against him, and he braced himself for the inevitable verdict.

The jury deliberated for hours before reaching a unanimous verdict guilty on all counts. The courtroom erupted in a mix of relief and satisfaction as the verdict was read aloud. Tyrone's family and supporters sat in stunned silence; their hopes dashed.

LIVING THAT LIFE

Chapter 10:

Sentencing

The judge, known for his tough stance on crime, delivered a stern sentencing. Tyrone was sentenced to 25 years in prison without the possibility of parole. The judge cited Tyrone's extensive criminal history and the severity of his crimes as factors in the harsh sentencing.

As Tyrone was led away in handcuffs, he cast one last glance at his family, his eyes filled with a mix of regret and determination. He vowed to himself that he would find a way to beat the system, no matter what it took.

Years passed, and Tyrone served his time in prison, biding his time and planning his next move. He became a model inmate, avoiding trouble and taking part in prison programs to prove his rehabilitation. His appeals for a reduced sentence were repeatedly denied, but he never gave up hope.

LIVING THAT LIFE

Chapter 11:

Release on Technicality

One day, Tyrone's lawyer visited him with surprising news. A technicality had been discovered in the original search warrant used to raid his house. The warrant had been improperly executed, and key evidence had been obtained illegally as a result. This technicality could be the key to Tyrone's release.

Tyrone's lawyer filed an appeal based on the technicality, and after a lengthy legal battle, the court ruled in Tyrone's favor. The evidence obtained from the illegal search warrant was considered inadmissible, and Tyrone's conviction was overturned. He was released from prison, a free man once again.

Tyrone's release from prison was met with a mix of joy and trepidation by his family and associates. While his return was celebrated, others were wary of his intentions and the potential trouble he might bring. Tyrone reassured them that he had changed, that prison had taught him the error of his ways, and that he was determined to live a law-abiding life.

However, old habits die hard, and unfortunately, Tyrone soon found himself drawn back into the world of crime. He reunited with his old crew, and together, they began planning new heists, determined to make up for lost time and reclaim their former glory.

LIVING THAT LIFE

Chapter 12:

Family and Friends

Years have begun passing by as relatives of Leroy and Marcus try to visit to show concern and hope to help them to stay strong as they serve their time. Leroy began going to Bible study in group sessions and eventually Marcus joined them.

As time went on, the faith of the two never strayed as they distanced themselves away from their loved ones to cope and help them stay sane.

After years had gone by, they had noticed that Tyrone was released already causing concern within Leroy. Leroy was worried that Tyrone would try to contact his wife Terri, the one person he had to stop communications within order to serve his time in peace. Leroy knew that he couldn't call Terri. And refused to reach out to Glenn, but he did have someone to reach out to, and it was James, his other brother-in-law. James began to be Leroy's eyes on the outside.

Leroy's marriage to Terri added a new layer of complexity to their already complicated relationship due to Glenn being the new Pastor of the church. Leroy's anger caused unwanted emotions to stay stirred up between his loyalty to his wife and his friendship with Glenn. This tension was palpable and created a sense of unease throughout the entire ordeal. As the situation unfolded, Terri found herself caught in the middle of the conflict between her husband and her brother. She struggled with conflicting emotions, torn between her love for Leroy and her loyalty to her family. After months of trying to visit or even write Leroy with no feedback, Terri felt that Leroy abandoned her and their kids. The family dynamic became even more strained as more time passed by, adding an extra layer of drama to an already tense situation. After a couple of years had gone by, Leroy stopped all communication with family while he was locked up. Marcus's release came sooner than expected, leaving Leroy alone for the rest of his days locked up. But Leroy eventually found allies that couldn't stand the ground that Tyrone walks on. They made mention that they wouldn't mind getting close to him at any given time. Leroy kept those words rooted in mind. He asked them to keep tabs on what Tyrone was up to since his release, and he asked James to keep eyes on his wife Terri. Leroy was scheduled to go up for parole again, but unlike the first couple of times, he was granted parole this time. He would have to spend six months in a halfway house in a city not too far from where he was from, called Austin, Texas. After another six months, he was able to go back to Temple.

LIVING THAT LIFE

Chapter 13:

Reunion at the Park

Eleven years had passed like a slow, relentless river. Leroy and Marcus found themselves back in the familiar surroundings of their old neighborhood, just a block away from the church. The basketball court was where they often gathered to reminisce and plan their next moves.

Leroy, his eyes distant, spoke first. "Those were long, tough years we served, man. Ten long years away from my wife and kids. My son was only three years old, and my daughter wasn't even born yet. It should've only been three years".

Marcus, leaning against the chain-link fence, replied, "Nobody told you to join the fight? I was doing just fine until I got hit from behind."

Leroy chuckled; a sound tinged with both amusement and regret. "Yeah, just fine until that lunch tray came across the back of your head. Then you were out, but I had to jump in when they started kicking and knocking your butt out. That's when I got involved, or you probably would not be here." Marcus nodded, remembering the incident vividly. "You ended up getting hurt too." Leroy's expression darkened as he said, "That's because as soon as I went to grab the one kicking you, the other guy grabbed me and threw me into the table headfirst. Then he took the edge of the tray and broke my arm in two places. So, because of you, I got a broken arm and eight more years. Every time you got into it with somebody, I seemed to get added time along with you. You owe me big time"! Marcus sighed saying, "a familiar argument. Man, why do I keep having to apologize time after time? And as far as Glenn, Pastor or not, he still owes me for leaving us out there." Marcus countered, "Glenn is not paying you a thang except a prayer for you to God." Leroy shook his head, "Naw, bro, he's going to pay, one way or another." Marcus countered, "Like I said, Glenn's not paying anything. Your payment is, you married his sister and got kids by her, so he owes you nothing". As he giggles. Leroy conceded slightly. "Well, maybe when you put it that way he doesn't, but you do".

Marcus looked at Leroy, his expression serious. "All I can say is thank you and I'm sorry for making all that noise during the burglary and for all the fights I got into. Thanks for having my back.

I've been noticing that for a whole year, we've come to this basketball court, and you've been watching Glenn's church every Sunday. At least I go inside for service. All you do is watch everybody. I know who you're watching, and if you want her back, your first step would be to show up at the church or go home. It's still your home too, she hasn't divorced you yet". Leroy gives Marcus a little smirk, as he hesitates to say, "If I do that, I'll run into Glenn, and I am not trying to see him right now."

Marcus pressed on. "Whatever, man. You're crazy. You want your family but aren't willing to do what it takes to get them. Leroy, you need to come to church with me today and at least try to make contact. Dude, you haven't even seen your own daughter yet. I see her every Sunday; she doesn't know me either, but I'm not the one she needs to know. And what about your son, who happens to be named after you? Man, if I had the chance to see my kids, I would love to, but they live out of state. Yours are right there in front of you. Come on, man."

Leroy's resolve wavered. "I don't know about this. What if…" Marcus cut him off. "What if she accepts you back? Won't it be worth the try? Talk to her; she might still be waiting for you. Of course, you should have done it a year ago, but it's never too late for God to work miracles. And as far as Glenn, he's the pastor now, so he's compelled to forgive or ask for forgiveness. As a matter of fact, he's tried to talk to you, but you won't let him. Maybe he's trying to apologize to you. He and I already settled our problem; you're the only one still holding onto it."

Leroy sighed, the weight of the past heavy on his shoulders. "Yeah, you're right. But it's hard letting go of something that cost me ten years of my life.," Marcus nodded understandingly. "Leroy, we all were at fault. Not just Glenn. I did the ten years with you, remember? There was one night about four months ago when I came to church. I was trying to push the door open to get in, but the usher wouldn't let me in." Leroy looked surprised. "What? Why?"

Marcus explained, "I found out later during the service, after she let me in, that nobody can walk in while the deacons or ministers are praying. But I forgot all about why I was so upset by the time church was out.

You see that usher's name was Yvonne Taylor. You remember from school, the Taylor sisters?" Leroy's eyes lit up with recognition. "Yeah, yeah, I think I know who you're talking about. Man, that girl was fine." Marcus smiled. "She still is bro. But after I finally got her to open up to me, we've been talking ever since."

Leroy raised an eyebrow. "So, let me get this straight. You aren't going to church to hear the preaching or the choir; you just want the girl. And you're trying to get me to do the same thing." Marcus laughed, "No, it's not the same thing because you are still married to the girl you want to see. You're the one holding up progress now. So, what are you going to do?" Leroy took a deep breath, his decision made. "Alright, I'm coming." With a newfound determination, Leroy and Marcus headed towards the church, ready to face the past and embrace the future.

LIVING THAT LIFE

Chapter 14:

Sunday Morning Service

Across town, Glenn Williams stood at the pulpit of Temple Community Church, his voice resonating with conviction. The congregation hung on his every word, their faces a mix of hope and reverence. Glenn's sermons were known for their passion and insight, drawing people from all walks of life. His wife, Vicki, sat in the front row, her eyes fixed on her husband as he spoke. She had come a long way from her flirtatious and loud past, now fully supportive of their ministry. Their children, Terrence, Denise, and Tracy, were all actively involved in the church, their talents shining brightly.

As the choir began to minister, the heavy wooden doors of the church creaked open, and Leroy and Marcus stepped inside. The air was filled with the harmonious voices of the choir, their melodies rising to the vaulted ceiling. The congregation was on their feet, swaying gently to the rhythm of the music.

"Who can change a hateful heart? Who can offer you a new start? Who can make a way out of no way? Who can change the words you say? Who can deliver a lost soul? Who is richer than silver and gold? Who can dry your weeping eyes? Who can distinguish an humble cry? All you need is Jesus, all you need is Jesus..."

The choir's voices softened as Pastor Williams stood at the podium, his presence commanding yet warm. "Praise the Lord saints," he began, his voice booming through the sanctuary. "I said, praise the Lord church! I hope you came for a Word from God this morning. Today is your day of deliverance, but it's up to you to open your heart and let Jesus in. I am here to tell you; all you need is Jesus!"

The choir echoed his words, their voices blending in perfect harmony. Pastor Williams continued, his voice filled with conviction. "Because He is all you will ever need, He is the planted seed in your life, He can change your hateful heart, and He will offer you a new start.

Leroy looked around the church, his eyes scanning familiar faces. He felt a tug in his heart, a mixture of guilt and longing. As the pastor's words resonated within him, he found himself standing up and walking towards the altar.

Pastor Williams noticed Leroy and smiled warmly. "My brother, I have been praying for you for some time now. I know you've been struggling with issues inwardly, and I believe that I am one of few issues that has kept you away. I want to publicly apologize to you, just like I did to Marcus. I hope you accept my apology. I truly am sorry for what happened between us years ago, but I know that my God is a forgiving God. He forgave me, and He'll forgive you. You took the first step when you came through those doors and instead of sitting down listening to the choir, you took another step and walked up to the altar, which shows that you are trying to change. It's not a long process, only if you don't forgive, not only others but yourself. Your family are here, and I believe they miss you, but the choice is in your hands. God brought you out not to sin but to mend what was broken."

The choir began singing softly, their voices filling the church with a melody of forgiveness and redemption. Leroy turned and walked back to his seat, his heart heavy with emotion.

After the service, Glenn greeted the congregation, his mother, Monica Williams—or Mama Williams, as everyone called her—by his side. She was a formidable presence, always ready with advice, whether asked for or not. Vicki, though grateful for her mother-in-law's support, often found herself irritated by Monica's constant interference.

"Glenn, you did wonderful today," Monica said, patting her son's arm. "But you need to speak more about the youth. They're the future of this church." Vicki rolled her eyes but said nothing, choosing to focus on the positive feedback from the congregation.

Meanwhile, Marcus stood at the back of the church, with his girlfriend Yvonne by his side. Yvonne, one of the ushers, greeted the congregation with a warm smile and her eyes lingering on Marcus with affection.

Marcus looked over where Leroy was standing out in the foyer and signaled to him with a nod and glanced toward Terri who was walking out of the church. Leroy saw his opportunity and approached Terri in the hallway; his voice tentative. "Terri, can I talk to you..." Terri's response was sharp and dismissive. "Not now, Leroy. You never wrote back to me or accepted my visits for ten long years, and now you come to church thinking it's all peaches and cream, but I don't work that way!" Their children, L.J. and a younger daughter, approached them, but Terri quickly ushered them away, leaving Leroy standing alone in the hallway. Pastor Williams, noticing the exchange, called Leroy into his office.

"Leroy, like I said in service, you will have to be patient," Pastor Williams began, his voice calm and reassuring. Leroy's frustration boiled over. "Patient? Man, patient! I've had ten years of patience. You can't be more patient than that!" Pastor Williams raised his hand, signaling for Leroy to calm down. "Leroy, settle down, please. We are still in the church." Leroy's voice was laced with bitterness. "Yeah, I see. You decided to hide and cover up your sins by calling yourself a so-called minister or, my bad, pastor."

Pastor Williams sighed; his eyes filled with remorse. "Leroy, I have tried to apologize to you several times while you were locked up and even since you've been out. I'm sorry that you think that I drove off and left you and Marcus at that house, I did think about doing that at first because I had a family to take care of, just like you did, but you both were taking too long. When I heard that noise, I didn't know what to do, so I started up the car and waited, but y'all didn't come out. And when I heard those sirens coming from a distance, I did what I..."

Leroy interrupted, his voice cold. "Yes, I know, you got scared as always. But this time, you being scared got Marcus and I locked up for ten years. You were also scared, even in school. I should've known better than to bring you along." Pastor Williams nodded, acknowledging Leroy's words. "I know, but now that I have accepted the Call of God, I am no longer scared to speak, especially when God gives me what to say. But back to that ten-year statement. You both only got three years of time. It was your own fault that caused you to stay seven years longer."

Leroy shook his head, his voice filled with regret. "No sir, it was Marcus doing. He couldn't keep his mouth shut and got into fights, but they were close calls that almost cost him his life. That's why I stepped in to defend him, just like I did when you got in some situations."

Pastor Williams chuckled, shaking his head. "Okay, Leroy, okay. I really thought that y'all would have gotten away like you did before. But anyway, we are having dinner at my house today, and I want to invite you to come out. Marcus already knows about it because we do this every first Sunday." Leroy hesitated; his voice was uncertain. "I don't know about that".

Pastor Williams leaned in; his voice conspiratorial. "I know I shouldn't say this, but Terri and the kids were also invited, so if you decide to come, you just may be able to talk to her privately and say what's on your mind." Leroy's eyes widened in surprise. "Well, oh man, I don't know... So, Terri's coming?" Pastor Williams nodded. "She was invited. I'm not sure if she will show up, but she normally does. I'm just saying that this may be your chance unless you're scared."

Leroy bristled at the suggestion. "Scared? Man, I don't normally get scared! But I will think about it. I do apologize for coming at you like I did. I did see a big difference in you today than I did eleven years ago. Because for you to even speak to me concerning Terri in front of the whole church was very bold. And I now know that it had to be God talking through you. And I hope what you said is true because I really want my family back."

Pastor Williams smiled; his eyes filled with hope. "So, are you coming or not?" Leroy nodded; his voice filled with determination. "Yeah, I mean yes, I will try to make it. I really hope Terri and the kids come too." As they began to walk out of the office, Pastor Williams called out to Leroy once more. "Oh, Leroy..." Leroy turned to face him. "What's up?"

Pastor Williams' voice was filled with gratitude. "Thank you and Marcus for not snitching on me and for not spreading it around the church or even the neighborhood. There are those who remember that I belonged here as a kid, and they have accepted me as their pastor, and I intend to be a vessel of God one hundred and ten percent. I owe you both, and that's one reason that I am eager to help you get back with Terri. But remember, she is my little sister, and I need you to do good by her." Leroy's voice was filled with sincerity. "Man, if you can help me get her back, I will do everything within my power to make her happy."

Pastor Williams nodded; his voice filled with understanding. "Okay my brother, and again I say thank you. I will see you at about 2:30 pm, right?" Leroy grinned. "Maybe about 3 pm." Pastor Williams smiled; his voice filled with warmth. "Cool…"

Leroy yelled out, "By the way", "What's on your mind, Leroy?" Glenn Responded. With a deep breath he says. "It's your brother James. He called this morning about something concerning Tyrone; I told him that I couldn't get involved due to being on probation. But I was just thinking maybe he could come to your house later after church. He's your brother, maybe you could talk to him too." Glenn's eyes softened. "Of course, Leroy. We'll help him together. Family sticks together, no matter what." I don't understand why he just doesn't come to talk to me anymore. Leroy's heart filled with gratitude as he said, "well Glenn, I kind of understand his position a little bit. I've had a hard time coming to you as he too, he giggled. I've come a long way from my days in prison, so with James being on the streets and you probably been preaching at him instead of ministering to him for years now. You must be a little more patient with us, and we know that we get love and support from our family and community. Leroy then glanced through the church doors and saw Officer Tisdale walking by and said, "Look who's lurking around outside". Pastor Williams said, Leroy, ignore him.

As they talked, Officer Gerald Tisdale walked by the church, his eyes scanning the neighborhood. He knew the streets of Temple like the back of his hand, and he had his sights set on Tyrone Jackson, who seemed to have his hands in every illegal deal. Tyrone, along with his crew—Mike Witherspoon and his younger brother Wesley—were a constant thorn in the side of the police department. Captain Allen Swinson, Tisdale's superior, had made it clear that bringing down Tyrone was a top priority. Tisdale nodded to himself, determined to make it happen.

LIVING THAT LIFE

Chapter 15:

A Family Gathering

The aroma of a home-cooked meal filled the air as Pastor Williams paced nervously around his living room. The clock read 2:45 pm, and the anticipation of the gathering weighed heavily on his mind. "Honey, is the food ready? I'm starving," he called out to his wife, Vicki, who was busy in the kitchen. Vicki's voice floated back, tinged with a hint of exasperation. "It's almost ready, dear. Why don't you go sit down and watch the game or something?" Pastor Williams hesitated, then called out again, "Baby..." Vicki sighed, "What is it, Glenn? I'm trying to finish cooking..." He took a deep breath before confessing, "I kind of invited Leroy over for dinner." There was a pause, and then Vicki's voice rose in surprise. "Leroy? Terri's husband?" "Yes, dear. Terri's husband," Pastor Williams confirmed, bracing himself for her reaction.

Vicki's voice grew stern. "Ooh, honey, what were you thinking? It's going to turn out to be a big mess. I don't want any junk in my house. Why didn't you just let God work it out for them?" She hurriedly began to put away sharp objects and glass. "I am not going to have blood on my hands and live with guilt like you've done for the past ten years. Wait just one minute. Is that what this is about? Your guilty feeling for taking Terri's husband from her and the kids?"

Pastor Williams nodded; his voice filled with remorse. "Yeah, kind of... Well, I've been feeling bad about it all, especially when Marcus first came to the ministry. I see how much happier he is since he came and started working at the church five months ago and even found a nice, godly lady friend. So, I figured, if God can change him, He will do the same for Leroy and Terri."

Vicki shook her head, her voice filled with concern. "But honey, that's different. Marcus and Yvonne just met months ago, after he changed his life. Leroy was married to Terri, and he knew what he was doing and the consequences for doing what he did back then. He could have decided not to go through with the robbery. You did; why couldn't he?"

Pastor Williams raised an eyebrow as he felt guilty because was involved. But he brushed it off by saying, "Well, first lady, I'm the pastor."

Vicki chuckled; her voice playful. "Well, mister, you weren't the pastor then, and since I am married to you, that makes me the pastor's wife, which makes me her first lady." Pastor Williams sighed. "Why didn't she go to Mama about it?" Vicki shrugged. "Glenn, she did try to, but all your mama would say is 'baby, pray on it.' Pastor Williams giggled. "Yep, that sounds just like Mama. Okay, I understand. I really believe that this will work. Being around family and getting a little food in your stomach always seems to help me cope with my problems." Vicki nodded, her voice softening. "That's how you do it; that doesn't work for everyone. Nobody wants to be around family every time they have a problem. But I hope it works, for your sake."

Pastor Williams' voice was filled with conviction. "I believe good will come out of it all. I felt a shift in his spirit this morning as I was ministering to him. His heart was beginning to soften up. That was a start to being delivered." Vicki looked at him, her eyes filled with concern. "You know he's still holding a grudge against you." Pastor Williams' eyes widened in surprise. "How do you know that?" Vicki smiled; her voice filled with pride. "You're not the only one with spiritual connections. Well, maybe this isn't spiritual connections, but I have connections too. Yvonne fills me in whenever she and Marcus get together."

Pastor Williams chuckled, shaking his head. "So, you got the ushers spying for you now? That's why I see them laughing sometimes and throwing up gang-like signs?" Vicki laughed, shaking her head. "It's not even like that, but he really wanted to get back at you, so be careful. I know God is working on him, but he isn't delivered from those thoughts in his head. He may want to be and try to be, but until he forgives you and himself, he won't truly be free." Pastor Williams nodded; his voice filled with awe. "Wow, that's exactly what I told him today. My God..."

Vicki smiled; her voice filled with love. "Like I said, I'm the pastor's wife, and I feel things that you go through, even when you are sleeping. I get up most times at 5 am and just start praying for God to strengthen you to keep on going. I know it's hard sometimes, but that's what a pastor's wife does. You preach to the church, and I pray for the church, and you are too." Pastor Williams' voice was filled with gratitude. "Thank you for being my boy... Let me get back to cooking before the food burns up or we'd be ordering takeout."

Pastor Williams nodded; his voice filled with hope. "Okay, dear. It sure does smell good too. You know, I believe Terri still loves Leroy." Vicki nodded; her voice filled with certainty. "I know she does. We talk just about every night. I guess this is your way of staying out of their business, huh? Well, if you ask me, you're all up in their business too." Pastor Williams chuckled, shaking his head. "Huh? Vicki don't be like that. It will work out. You'll see."

The doorbell rang, and Vicki called out from the kitchen, "Honey, get the door, I'm trying to prepare dinner." Pastor Williams opened the front door to find his son, Terrence, standing on the other side. "Hey son, I enjoyed the music today as always." Terrence smiled, as he walked inside. "Hey Dad, thanks. We had a few issues at rehearsal, but we finally ironed them out before today's service." Pastor Williams nodded; his voice filled with pride. "Well, you couldn't tell anything was wrong. They sounded great as they sang under the anointing. You know that does make a difference." Terrence nodded; his voice filled with agreement. "I believe that, because what I heard at rehearsal, compared to today, you would think it was a totally different choir."

Vicki walked out from the kitchen; her voice filled with warmth. "Hello son, enjoyed your music, boy you really played well as usual." Terrence smiled as his eyes lit up saying, "Soon I'll have some help when L.J. gets a few more piano lessons under his belt. He's coming along pretty good. Mom... it sure does smell good here."

Pastor Williams chuckled, his voice playful. "Oh thanks, Terrence, that's my new cologne." Vicki rolled her eyes, laughing. "Glenn stops playing, he's talking about the food." Pastor Williams grinned, his voice filled with humor. "I knew that. But you must admit, I do smell good," Terrence's expression suddenly grew serious. "Dad, I almost forgot... I saw Uncle Leroy and Uncle James up the street about half an hour ago. I started to speak to them, but just as I started toward them, then I saw Tyrone pull up. So, I watched them for a little while. Tyrone pulled Uncle Leroy to the side and started talking to him. But everything looked okay, so I came on to the house to eat." Pastor William's face expression suddenly changed as his voice filled with remorse. "My God... Oh Jesus... Terrence's eyes widened in alarm. "Dad what's wrong?"

Pastor Williams took a deep breath, his voice filled with remorse. "I know you probably don't know this, but about eleven years ago, I did a job with Tyrone along with Leroy and Marcus. That's why they ended up doing the time that they did. It was my fault. I was the getaway driver. I didn't tell your mom the whole story. She thinks that I was supposed to be with them as the getaway driver but chickened out. She doesn't know the truth, that I broke in the house with them and went through the window too. This is so embarrassing to talk about, even now as a Pastor.

Pastor Williams took another deep breath, his voice filled with remorse. "I heard a noise in the living room area where Marcus was that scared me, and when I heard Leroy say run, I took off running out the door. I ran to the car thinking Leroy and Marcus were behind me, but when I looked back, I saw them running the opposite way. So, I went on and hid in the car while waiting. I didn't know Leroy was over there fussing at Marcus instead of running. But he blames us for getting caught. But anyways, I heard sirens from a distance, so I yelled for them to come on, but they didn't hear me. I figured that I'd wait a little longer. I finally saw them running thinking they would make it to the car, but suddenly, as they were running towards me, two cops pulled up on them yelling. When I saw those cops pull their guns and force them to the ground, I did what anybody would have done and ducked down until it was clear hoping that I wasn't spotted. The cops never looked over to where I was, and even though they were caught, they never said that I was right there in the car not too far behind them. So, I was able to get away. I am grateful that neither Leroy nor Marcus snitched on me, and I am so grateful to them for that. But I think that Tyrone was talking to Leroy about some money that was taken from one of his boys prior to us doing the robbery." Terrence replied, "Wow dad, which was too intense for me!" Glenn giggled saying, "Yes it was and unfortunately, still is just talking about it."

The doorbell rang again, and Pastor Williams held up a finger. Terrence, "Hold on a second, let me get to the door right quick." He opened the door to find Terri standing on the other side, her eyes filled with warmth. "Hey, Terri, I am glad you came." Terri smiled, stepping inside. "Hey big brother, man you really ministered to me this morning. I don't know if anyone else received it, but I did." Pastor Williams nodded; his voice filled with hope. "So have you given what I talked about any thought?" Terri nodded; her voice filled with certainty. "Yes, Glenn, I have and still doing a little thinking." Pastor Williams' voice was filled with understanding. "That's good but take your time. You have to think about your kids too."

Terri nodded, her eyes scanning the room. "I know and I will. Where is Vicki?" Pastor Williams gestured toward the kitchen saying, "She's in the kitchen getting the food prepared. Go ahead, I believe she needs help. I already told her that I was hungry, but she's taking her sweet old time." He chuckled as Terri made her way to the kitchen.

"Hey, Terri, can I help you?" Vicki's voice was filled with relief. "Girl, yes, it's taking a little longer to cook today, grab something and start working". Her eyes filled with concern as she looked at Terri. "Terri, are you okay?" Terri nodded; her voice filled with certainty. "Yes, I am fine. I just have a lot to think about." Vicki's voice filled with understanding. "Is it Leroy? Terri nodded; her voice filled with longing. "Yes, Vicki, it's Leroy. I want to let him back in to my heart, but it's been so long, I just don't know. He doesn't even know his own kids." Vicki's voice was filled with wisdom. "Well, sis, don't you think he deserves a chance? At least meet them."

Terri nodded; her voice filled with uncertainty. "Yes, I know. That's mainly what I've been worried about. I don't know how they will react to him, especially

Larissa. She wasn't even born yet when he left." Vicki's voice was filled with encouragement. "If I were you, I would at least talk with him one on one." Terri nodded; her voice filled with agreement. "Yes, I know. That's what I've been worried about. I don't know where he lives. Where in the world will we talk other than at church? It's too soon to go out; And I'm surprised he hasn't tried to come to the house, legally, it's still partly his house too, but I'm glad that he hasn't pushed that issue, I wouldn't be comfortable for that yet." Vicki chuckled; her voice filled with amusement.

"Terri, I am about to tell you something, but you promise you won't leave." Terri's eyes widened in alarm. "What is it, Vicki?" Vicki took a deep breath, her voice filled with hesitation. "How can I say this? Glenn invited Leroy over for dinner today." Terri's voice rose in alarm. "What? No... Not now... Vicki's voice was filled with reassurance. "Hold on now, didn't you say you were open to talking to him? Hold on, I just heard the doorbell". "Well, is it him"? Terri asked. Vicki says, "Girl, hold on, I'm trying to see." Pastor Williams opened the front door, his voice filled with warmth saying, "Hey ladies, I'm glad you finally made it." Terri's voice was filled with alarm. "Who is it?" Vicki's voice was filled with relief. "You can stop pouting now; it's my girls, Denise and Tracy. It looks like L.J. and Larissa came in with them." Terri's voice was filled with relief. "Okay... I'm fine now. They asked if they could hang out with your daughters today and meet over here". Vicki's voice was filled with amusement. "I surely hope so, cause girl, you were a wreck a while ago."

Denise's voice floated in from the living room, filled with enthusiasm. "Hello Daddy, where's the food? I'm hungry." Tracy's voice was filled with warmth. "Hey Daddy, what's up, Terrence?" Pastor Williams' voice was filled with pride. "Hey kids! come on in, mama is in the kitchen. Go help her get that food out here." Larissa's voice was filled with excitement. "Hello, Uncle Glenn." Pastor Williams smiled; his voice filled with warmth. "Hey! There's my little girl, how are you doing? Hey L.J., have you learned any new music yet?" L.J.'s voice filled with confidence saying, "It's coming along just fine. It's pretty easy."

Pastor Williams' voice suddenly grew concerned. "Wait a minute, where's Mama? Didn't y'all pick her up?" Tracy's voice was filled with confusion. "No Daddy, we thought she was already here." Pastor Williams' voice was filled with alarm. "Oh Lord, we left Mama at the church. I'll be back. Maybe she's still there." He hurried to the door, but as he reached for the handle, it swung open to reveal his mother standing on the other side. "Mama! I was about to come get you. How did you get here?" Mama Williams' voice was filled with amusement. "Boy hush and let me in. Hey y'all, is the food ready yet?"

Pastor Williams chuckled to himself; his voice filled with amusement. "Lord, and I thank you for the humor that my mom brings into my life." He called out to her; his voice filled with agreement. "Yes, Mama, I'm coming... We all went into the dining room as Pastor Williams blessed the food. Everyone sat down and began to eat, the atmosphere filled with a sense of unity and love. After the meal, Pastor Williams gathered

Leroy and James in the living room, his expression serious. "Let's get this straight," he began, his voice firm. "I am not going to do anything that causes harm to anyone. Are we straight?" Leroy nodded, his voice filled with agreement. "Yes, we're straight..."

Pastor Williams turned to James; his voice filled with concern. "James, what about you?" As he laid his hands upon James' shoulders. James snatched his shoulder away from Glenn saying, "Look, I called and talked with Leroy earlier today concerning Tyrone. But he said we'll meet about my concerns after church. But before we could meet, Tyrone saw us up in the street not too long ago before I could meet with both of you. While I was in the store, he approached Leroy about dealing with him for something I did against him and one of his guys. I took the money that was taken. I am not trying to involve anyone else in my mess", his voice filled with defiance. They all looked at each other nodding, as James continued saying, "But yeah man, I hear you, but I will do what I have to do." As he walked off, left the room.

Leroy walked James to the front door. As he watched with a thoughtful expression saying, "Glenn... He'll be okay... He told me that he was worried about Terri and that he would do anything to protect his little sister. I can understand how he feels, because I feel the same way. I lost Terri once, and sitting there today eating dinner, I watched how she enjoyed being around you all. I want her to feel that way toward me again. I need to talk to her; will you please help me..."

Pastor Williams nodded, his voice filled with understanding. "Yes, Leroy, I see that you really want to make things work between you and Terri, so I don't mind helping you. But you must make better decisions... She's also my little sister too." Leroy nodded, his voice filled with determination. "I hear you, Pastor Glenn, I hear...as he giggled. Pastor Williams called out to Terri; his voice filled with request. "Hey Terri, come here for a minute. "I'm in the living room". Terri entered the room, her eyes widening slightly as she saw Leroy. "Glenn, what is it?" Pastor Williams gestured to Leroy; his voice filled with encouragement. "Terri, if you are willing, Leroy would like to speak with you..." Terri hesitated before nodding, her voice soft. "Oh... okay..." Pastor Williams looked at Leroy, his voice filled with support. "Well, Leroy, here's your chance..." He left the room, giving them space to talk. Leroy took a deep breath; his voice filled with urgency. "Thanks, Glenn... Terri, I..." Terri started to speak, but Leroy interrupted her, his voice filled with pleading. "Hold on, Terri, before you go off. This was Glenn's idea, and..." Terri's eyes narrowed; her voice filled with suspicion. "Glenn's idea? So, are you saying you didn't want to come?"

Leroy shook his head; his voice filled with sincerity. "No, baby, no... That's not what I am saying... I did want to come, and I would have been here sooner, but James and I got caught up... Terri's voice was filled with frustration. "Yeah, yeah, always an excuse. Leroy's voice was filled with desperation. "Terri, listen to me, please. I've missed you every day for the past eleven years, and I had made up my mind that today, I was going to step up and do what I should have done a year ago when I was released. Please forgive me. Terri's voice was filled with doubt. "I don't know, Leroy... We were married, and still are, but you should have come home a year ago when you were released. At least then, maybe I could have forgiven you. But you were released a whole year ago and you never called, came by, or even tried to write to me. You have two kids, and one of them you never even seen before today."

Leroy's voice was filled with regret. "I know, but... Terri's voice was firm. "But nothing, Leroy... Do you know the number of chances that I had to move on with my life, but I didn't, trying to wait on you, and for what? You never wrote back to me after your first six months of being locked up. I met men that wanted to go out with me, but I was waiting and waiting until... Terri's voice was filled with pain. "Never mind Leroy, it doesn't even matter anymore. I've survived, and I am moving forward. You did what you did, and now you know what was done to me. So now that we are discussing this, I think it is a good start to our healing process." Leroy nodded; his voice filled with agreement. "Yes, this is a good start, but I need to know what was done to me."

Terri shook her head, her voice filled with determination. "We can discuss it later in a more private location. Let me get the kids so you can at least have a chance to know them." She called out to the children, her voice filled with warmth. "L.J., get Larissa and y'all come here for a minute." The kids entered the room, their eyes curious as they looked at Leroy. Terri gestured to Leroy; her voice filled with introduction. "Larissa, meet your daddy." Leroy smiled; his voice filled with wonder. "Hi, Larissa, you are so beautiful..."

Larissa smiled shyly, her voice soft. "Thank you..." Leroy turned to L.J., his voice filled with emotion. "Hey there, L.J. I haven't seen you since you were about three years old. How are you doing?" L.J.'s voice was polite but distant. "I'm fine." The children left the room to go outside, leaving Leroy and Terri alone once more. Terri's voice was filled with apology. "I'm sorry about that, Leroy. It's going to take some time for them to get used to you being around." Leroy nodded; his voice filled with understanding. "I know, Terri... They are big kids... I really missed out on being here with them."

Terri's voice was filled with reflection. "Yes, you did miss a lot of great moments, but hopefully, things will work out. I really love them both, and I couldn't have made it this far without them in my life. L.J. was only three years old when you left, and Larissa wasn't even born yet." Leroy's voice was filled with hope. "I know it will take some time for them to get used to me, but can we start off by you agreeing to meet me for breakfast in a couple of days or so?" Terri nodded; her voice filled with agreement. "I think I can arrange that. Just call me later, and we will see about it... Leroy's voice was filled with gratitude. "Will do, will do... Thank you, Terri, for having an open mind... Terri's voice was filled with wisdom. "Well, Mama raised us to be open-minded about our situations. I am willing to do this work if you can do the same." Leroy's voice was filled with determination. "I am sure I am willing also, Terri... I'll call you tomorrow, okay?" Terri nodded; her voice filled with agreement. "Okay... I'll be waiting." Leroy left the room as Terri went to the kitchen to help

Vicki with the dishes, her mind filled with thoughts of the future.

LIVING THAT LIFE

Chapter 16:

Leroy and Terri Dating

Weeks had passed, and Leroy, Terri, and the kids had been spending time together. They enjoyed movies, dining out, and visiting amusement parks, rekindling the bond that had been lost over the years. Leroy felt a sense of renewal, a feeling he hadn't experienced in a long time.

"I feel like a new man!" Leroy exclaimed; his voice filled with joy. "I'm back with my family, and Glenn asked me if I was ready to get back into ministry. I just feel so good today... Terri smiled, her eyes reflecting a mix of happiness and curiosity. Leroy, I'm glad you're feeling so good, I was upset when you did what you did, but Glenn gave me his side of the story. Now, I want to know your side."

Leroy took a deep breath, his expression turning serious as he began to recount the events that led to his and Marcus's imprisonment. He spoke of the desperation, the poor decisions, and the regret that followed. "Okay, now you know what happened, and that's all in the past now."

Terri's voice was soft, tinged with a hint of sadness. "I wish it had never happened; you probably would've never stopped moving forward in ministry. You could have been a great pastor or even an evangelist by now."

Leroy nodded; his voice filled with remorse. "Yes, I know, I messed up big time, but I'm here now. We had

L.J, and you were pregnant again, and I felt like I wasn't making enough money. Instead of praying, I acted on my own thoughts and got your brother involved. I thank God that he was able to get away; he probably wouldn't be where he is now."

Terri's eyes in surprise. "Who? It was Glenn, at least until he ran to the getaway car leaving me and Marcus stranded." Terri's voice was filled with confusion. "Well, Glenn's story was a little different from yours. He said that everything went well until he heard a noise in the living room and you said run. He said he ran towards the car and when he looked back, you and Marcus were running in the other direction, and you started arguing with Marcus instead of running. This is what Marcus told him. Then you both ran after y'all heard the sirens, but it was too late."

Leroy sighed; his voice filled with resignation. "Well, Terri, I guess we all remember it differently. I thought you might have found out about it by now. But that's in the past now. It's all good because I am happy now that I am back in the lives of L.J. and Larissa and especially in your life, baby. This is a great feeling."

LIVING THAT LIFE

Chapter 17:

A New Dawn

The sun had barely risen over the horizon, casting a golden hue over the modest neighborhood of Temple. Leroy Mathis stood in his small kitchen, the aroma of freshly brewed coffee filling the air. His hands, calloused from years of hard labor, gripped the counter as he stared out the window, lost in thought.

Since his release from prison, every day there had been a struggle to provide for his family. The weight of his past mistakes hung heavy on his shoulders, but he was determined to make amends.

"Good morning, Leroy." Terri says as she enters the kitchen, her voice soft but firm. She placed a gentle hand on his back, her touch a reminder of the unwavering support she offered. "You up early again?"

Leroy turned to her, forcing a smile. "Just thinking about the day ahead. I finally have a job interview at the warehouse downtown." Terri's eyes lit up with hope. "Leroy, That's great. You'll do fine. Just stay focused."

The sound of piano keys echoed from the living room, where their son, L.J., was practicing. The 15-year-old had a natural talent for music, his fingers dancing over the keys with a grace that belied his age. "Morning, Mom, Dad," L.J. called out, not missing a beat. Larissa, their 11-year-old daughter, bounded into the kitchen, her curly hair bouncing with each step. "Morning!" she chirped, before playfully poking L.J. in the side. "You're always playing that thing." L.J. rolled his eyes but couldn't help smiling. "One day, I'm going to be a famous pianist, and you'll be sorry you bothered me." Terri laughed, shaking her head. "Alright, you two. Breakfast is ready. Leroy, you better eat something before you head out."

As they sat down to eat, the phone rang. Terri answered it, her expression turning serious. "It's your brother," she mouthed to Leroy, handing him the phone. Leroy took a deep breath before answering. "James, what's up?" His voice was tense. "Leroy, I need to talk to you. I heard that Tyrone was going to roll up on you unexpectedly saying something about seeing his little girl, but don't say anything, just act casual, I'm on my way." Leroy's grip tightened on the phone. "Alright, James. I'm on my way to an interview but come by the house later and we'll finish talking. "I'll have my package on me too, and probably load up some more just in case, if you know what I mean." James replied.

As he hung up, Leroy looked at Terri, who nodded encouragingly. "He needs you, Leroy. You can help him. Leroy smiled and nodded his head yes, but laughing in his thoughts saying he's the one that's always packing, we need him. Terry asked, did you say something Leroy?" "No. I didn't say anything Terri. I was just talking to myself." Leroy got in his car and went to his interview.

LIVING THAT LIFE

Chapter 18:

Surprise Visit

Hours passed by as Terri spent the day with the kids. Terri's expression suddenly changed; a worried look crossed her face as she thought about how to tell Leroy about something that she wished had never happened.

Leroy returns home with hope that he got the job, but then he saw a worried look on Terri's face, with concern, he asks, "Baby what's the matter?" Terri hesitated; her voice filled with uncertainty. "I have something to tell you. Leroy said with concern, "What is it honey?

Before Terri could continue, James knocked on the door, interrupted them, his voice filled with excitement. "Hey, Leroy... Come outside"

Terri's voice was filled with frustration. "James, we are in the middle of a serious conversation". James ignored Terri, his voice filled with enthusiasm. "Come outside now, come on Terri, it's not often that I have money to buy my niece ax "Look, I bought this keyboard for C.J. at the pawn shop, what do you think"?

Leroy nodded; his voice filled with approval. "Yeah, James, this is nice... I know he'll dig this... Come on, Terri, let's go give it to him. I can't wait to see his face."

James held another item, his voice filled with excitement. "Wait a minute, Leroy. I got Larissa something too. Check this out... I found this iPad for Larissa too... James began to say, "After we hung up earlier, I fell asleep, and I had a crazy dream. It felt so real I woke up yelling, no, stop!" Terri asked, "Are you okay? James said, "As a matter of fact, I feel great". "I'm focused. After we hung up, Glenn had called me back and started ministering to me. Now if y'all need to talk, we can still talk though", as James said jokingly.

As they were admiring the gifts, Tyrone pulled up and began to walk towards Leroy, his presence casting a shadow over the joyful moment.

"Well, well, well... What's up, Leroy?" Tyrone greeted, his eyes lingering on Terri. "Terri, you are as beautiful as ever..."

Leroy's voice was firm, his eyes narrowing. "What do you want, Tyrone?"

Tyrone chuckled; his voice filled with amusement. "Oh, you get right to the point, I like that. Tyrone's eyes flicked to Larissa, as he giggled saying. "And I heard you referring to your little girl. Larissa, right? You mean you haven't told him yet Terri? Wow! Well, Leroy, I have bad news for you. Tell my little girl I said hello."

Terri's voice was filled with desperation. Stop it, Tyrone! Come on, Leroy, let's go. Leroy's voice was filled with confusion. "Wait a minute Terri, what's he talking about? His little girl?

Tyrone laughed; his voice filled with malice. "That's right, Leroy, while you were gone, Terri was a little busy. Leroy dropped his head, his eyes filled with disbelief and anger. How did Larissa come about? All I know is she couldn't possibly be yours, Leroy.

About two to three months after we were arrested, it took them a little longer to find me, but they finally did. My trial lasted a good while and I was granted bail. I couldn't go home because it was being watched. So, I decided to see how my good old friend Terri was doing. So, I laid low right here until my trial date came about. She just happened to have a mishap, I just happened to be at the right place at the right time. Terri was going through an upset, just downright frustrated... so me, being the man that I am, gave her something she needed... Me! You weren't here, so somebody has to step in. And that's how Larissa got here... Leroy dropped his head, his eyes filled with disbelief and amazement as he looked at Terri asking, "Terri Is this true"?

Tyrone began his voice filled with malice and laughter. "Of course it's true... except, she didn't give it up freely; She had a little help that made her too weak to fight back." Terri's voice was filled with shame. "That's what I was trying to tell you, Leroy. Tyrone. He beat me, Leroy. He beat me so badly that I lost our baby. I had a miscarriage."

Leroy looked at Terri, his voice filled with disbelief. "What does he mean you lost my baby girl? With anger in his voice, Answer me, Terri!" Terri held her head downward, her eyes filled with shame. Leroy's voice was filled with confusion.

Tyrone leaned against his car, a smirk playing on his lips. "By the way Leroy, that money that James owes to me was partially paid today by your nephew. But I still need him and the rest of you to do right about the new agreement that Terrence made with me earlier. And just to reassure that I was serious, we had to rough him up a little... you may want to check the hospitals... He giggled and got into his car, driving off and leaving Leroy and Terri standing in stunned silence.

Leroy stood there watching Tyrone drive down the street almost in tears. Terri went to hug him, but Leroy pushed her off saying, "I need some air to think" and got in his car and drove off. Terri said "This is too much at one time James, let's go find Terrence... I'll talk to Leroy about Tyrone later".

Two hours later, Terrence was released from the emergency room, his face bruised and swollen. As he left the hospital, Terri and James rushed in, their eyes scanning the area for him.

Terri approached the nurse's station, "Excuse me, nurse... We're looking for my brother, Terrence Williams? We heard he may have been brought here." The nurse looked up from her desk, her professional voice. "Mr. Williams was released a little while ago.

While Terri and James went to the hospital, Leroy ended up hanging at Marcus house and instead of going home, Terrence also found himself heading over to talk with Marcus. He found him at his usual spot working on his car, with a surprised expression saying, "Hey,

Marcus, oh, hey Uncle Leroy, you're just the person I've been looking for. Terrence sighed; his voice filled with resignation. "Tyrone Turner called himself teaching me a lesson today". He said tell you and James that he wants his money by 11pm tonight. He said he was sending you both a message by beating me down and sending me to the ER. I spent 3 hours in the hospital".

Marcus' voice was filled with disbelief. "What? Why are you even dealing with Tyrone alone? It will never come out victorious. Do your family know about this?" Terrence shook his head, his voice filled with determination. "No, but I'm sure that probably only you and Leroy know." He started to walk off, but Marcus stopped him saying, "Where are you going? This is a serious matter. We can't allow you to go anywhere until we find out what's going on. I thought James got out of the street life?" Terrence nodded; his voice filled with explanation. "He did, but Tyrone didn't give them a choice. That's why I tried to help out. But Uncle Leroy, Tyrone said that he wanted to include you and my dad in the deal now that I've gotten involved.

The phone rang, Marcus answered it, "hello" his voice filled with urgency. "Hello, It's James, Hey, James, what's going on?" Marcus's voice was filled with concern. "I can't explain it right now; I'm looking for Terrence." Marcus nodded; his voice filled with reassurance. "He's here with us." James asked, "who's us"? Leroy grabbed the phone saying," Hey James this Leroy, Terrence is with me and Marcus. Is Terri with you? James replied, "yes, but her phone just rung, hold on".

Hey Leroy, we got a big problem! Terri just got a call from Tyrone. He has Larissa at his place by the park. He said since my nephew interfered, he wants his money today, or he's keeping Larissa." Leroy's voice was filled with desperation. "Lord, I can't go back to my old ways! We've got to do something." Marcus' voice was filled with confusion. "What are you talking about?" Leroy's voice was filled with urgency. "Terri just told me Tyrone has Larissa! Marcus, you and Terrence Go ahead and meet us at the park by the church." Marcus nodded; his voice filled with agreement. "Who's us?" Leroy's voice was filled with determination. "Terri, you and James meet us over at park by the church. I'll be there soon.

Leroy, Terri, James, Terrence, and Marcus met at the park to discuss how to get Larissa back. Leroy turned to Terri; his voice filled with urgency. "Terri, go ahead and call your brother. They should be finished eating by now. Tell him what's going on." Terri hesitated; her voice filled with reluctance. "I don't want to involve him. He has the church to think about." James' voice was filled with insistence. "Terri, Glenn needs to know what Terrence has gotten us into."

Terrence's voice was filled with defensiveness. "Me? Y'all are the ones that owe Tyrone all that money." Leroy started to speak, but Terri interrupted him with her voice filled with urgency, "I still want you to hear this from my mouth! Larissa is not,"... But Leroy interrupted her saying, "Terri, you and Terrence stay here and call your brother, Glenn. Marcus and James, come with me. I guess we have to do this our way, hopefully Glenn will get the police in time.

Marcus' voice was filled with concern. "Wait a minute, we don't have any guns or weapons." James' voice was filled with confidence. "Speak for yourself, man, I keep mine on me.   Leroy's voice was filled with surprise. "Terri, what are you doing? You going to mess around and get caught." Just as Leroy spoke, Terri was spotted...

Terri was escorted along with Terrence to Tyrone's office to wait for him. Tyrone got word that he had visitors. Tyrone approached his office and looks in the window saying, "what do we have here?" He peeps in the door and sees Terri trying to fight her way out, so he says, "take her out of my office before she knocks over my precious items.

   Leroy and James saw what was going on, but they were outnumbered and helpless. James decided to call in reinforcements. Leroy said, "Who are you calling" James responded, "we need help Leroy! My guns are no match for them. Dang, nobody's answering. I'm going to try to get closer. Leroy said, "don't get caught".

Glenn knew what they were up against and had contacted the police to let them know what was going on. He then discreetly left his house, unseen by anyone. He approached Tyrone's shop, as nervous as he was eleven years earlier during their robbery. Glenn approached the guys standing outside of the shop, asking to talk with Tyrone. Tyrone refused to come out, so they roughed the pastor up and told him to leave before he got dealt with. By this time, Marcus had found Larissa tied up but unharmed. He met with Leroy and

James, and Leroy hugged Larissa firmly, relieved to see that she was unharmed.

The police finally showed up outside, but Glenn intercepted them before they could force their way in. He told them that Terri, Larissa, and Terrence were being held against their will. The police waited for the detective in charge and his chief to show up before they approached the building. One of the guys outside the shop ran inside to warn Tyrone about the police setting outside. Tyrone had done years in prison already and wasn't planning on going back in.

Suddenly, a noise echoed from across the shop, causing Tyrone to send his men to investigate. Tyrone knew it could be Leroy, and a smirk played on his lips as he began to blurt out the truth he had been holding back. "That little girl, Larissa, is not your daughter, Leroy! I'm her daddy. What do you think about that Leroy!" Huh? Terri, still sitting on the ground, started crying out, "No, that's not how I wanted you to find out." Her voice was filled with anguish and regret.

Leroy, in a state of shock and amazement, began to stand up. He had accidentally bumped against a box of tools, causing noise that alerted everyone. As he rose, Tyrone grabbed Terri and slapped her hard across the face, causing her to fall to the ground. Larissa, seeing the scene, yelled out, "Mama!" as she stood up, her eyes wide with fear. Leroy reached for Larissa, but as he did, Tyrone fired a shot in their direction. The bullet struck Larissa in the right side of her chest, and she crumpled to the ground. Chaos erupted as James started shooting at Tyrone, prompting the rest of the gang to return fire.

The police stormed in, adding to the cacophony of gunshots.

When the dust settled, Larissa lay unconscious, a gunshot wound in her chest. Leroy and Terri held her tightly, their faces etched with worry and fear. Tyrone and four of his crew members were also shot, their bodies slumped on the floor.

LIVING THAT LIFE

Chapter 19:

Terri's Secret

One month later, the atmosphere was tense and uncertain. Larissa remained in critical condition, fighting for her life after the gunshot wound inflicted by Tyrone Turner, her biological father. Leroy and Terri were by her side, their faces worn with exhaustion and worry. Leroy left and had taken time away to clear his mind but returned to find his family in turmoil.

As they sat by Larissa's bedside, Terri turned to Leroy, her eyes filled with tears. "Leroy, there's something you need to know. Before you went to prison, I was pregnant with your child. But Tyrone... he beat me, Leroy. He beat me so badly that I lost our baby. I had a miscarriage." Leroy's face paled, his eyes widening in horror. "Terri... why didn't you tell me?" Terri's voice was filled with pain. "I couldn't, Leroy. I was ashamed and hurt. And then, weeks later, Tyrone... he raped me, Leroy. He drugged me and took advantage of me. That's how Larissa was conceived. Leroy, she's not your daughter, She's Tyrone's." Leroy's face darkened with fury. "Tyrone will pay for this, Terri. He will pay for every ounce of pain he's caused you."

Tyrone had survived the shooting but was now facing charges of attempted murder against his own daughter. The court proceedings were brutal, with witnesses recounting the horrific events of that day. James, who had acted in self-defense, was also entangled in the legal system, his fate hanging in the balance. Leroy, consumed by rage, plotted with Marcus to get even with Tyrone, even if it meant going through prison walls. They visited a fellow inmate in prison, their conversations laced with tension and unspoken threats against Tyrone. Tyrone, even from behind bars, seemed to hold a power over them all, his influence like a dark shadow.

Meanwhile, Leroy and Terri struggled to keep their family together. L.J. was distant, his music a solace but also a barrier between him and his parents. The church, once a place of solace, was now a reminder of the pain and betrayal they had endured. Pastor Glenn and Victoria did their best to support the family, but the weight of the tragedy was heavy on everyone. Marcus, trying to stay on the straight and narrow, found himself pulled back into the chaos. Glenn and James, despite their reservations, agreed to support Leroy in whatever he decided to do, bound by loyalty and the shared pain of their past.

Chapter 20:

The Paths Converge

As the days leading up to Tyrone's court proceedings approached, each character found themselves on a collision course with destiny. Leroy, fueled by vengeance, continued to orchestrate his plan from the shadows, ensuring that the inmate he hired was ready to strike at the opportune moment.

Meanwhile, Terri struggled with her emotions, torn between her love for Leroy and the fear of what was to come. She spent her days at Larissa's side, praying for strength and guidance. Glenn, determined to keep his family and community united, poured his heart into his sermons. His messages of forgiveness and redemption resonated through the church, rallying support and offering solace to those in need. He visited Leroy and Terri often, offering his unwavering support and guidance as they navigated the tumultuous waters ahead.

James, caught in the crossfire of loyalty and law, found himself in a precarious position. He sought Glenn's counsel, desperate to find a way to make amends and secure his future. His nights were filled with restless sleep, his mind racing with the possibilities of what lay ahead.

Marcus, ever the loyal friend, stood by Leroy's side, determined to see Tyrone brought to justice. He visited Tyrone in prison from a distance just to see who he has around him, working for and visiting him. Sometimes

Marcus would approach Tyrone at a face-to-face visit, their conversations laced with tension and unspoken threats. His past pulled him back into the shadows, but his loyalty to Leroy remained unwavering.

Amidst the chaos, one person remained overlooked. From the beginning he saw the events unfolding from day one, the memories of the past fueling a quiet rage within him. He had been plotting his own revenge against Tyrone. He keeps his thoughts to himself but every now and then, he'll release his plans to one other person just to keep his sanity. When he discovered Leroy's plan to hire a killer, he decided to take matters into his own hands. He visited Larissa in the hospital to check on her and then for his plan to work, he had been confiding in one other person to help devise a scheme. The last key needed was one of James' guns to make their move on the day of Tyrone's court date.

Chapter 21:

The Day of Reckoning

There was an opening that had drapes covering the entrance for decorations. The windows and the doors also had them. There was one side door that's not for the public, but perfect for someone to sneak into.

It was 9am, Tyrone's court date arrived, and the atmosphere was electric. Larissa had been home and recovering for weeks now. She wanted to go to the hearing, so she called Uncle James, but he didn't answer, but she managed to find a ride. She was the center of the case of Mathis vs Turner. The judge listened to the arguments;

On the outside of the courtroom two individuals were reported coming through an unauthorized area, they had snuck into the side hallway of the courtroom, hiding in the area where Tyrone would be entering through a side door. Their plan was to strike at the same time as the hired shooter, ensuring that Tyrone would face justice. However, unknown to them, a line of inmates was escorted down the hall at the same time, two of whom were part of Tyrone's crew, the weight of the decision heavy on his shoulders. As the judge prepared to deliver his verdict, a sudden commotion outside the courtroom disrupted the proceedings.

As the hired shooter made his move, one of the members of Tyrone's crew recognized him and yelled for Tyrone to get down. The shooter, startled, accidentally shot a guard and one of the prisoners. The guard returned fire, striking the shooter as he turned to flee. In the chaos, Tyrone reached for the guard's gun and began shooting at the shooter. He then saw movement from his righthand side coming from around the wall as he was shooting. He then pointed his gun towards where he had previously seen the movement but then suddenly saw a gun pointing directly at him. But L.J., frozen in fear, dropped his gun as the scene unfolded before him. Tyrone saw the gun fall to the floor as he glanced back down the hall to see if anyone else was coming for him. Larissa, however, was consumed by a sudden flashback of the moment Tyrone shot her. As Tyrone stood and looked back towards his right with a smirk playing on his lips, he looked eye to eye with his daughter as they stared at each other. Everything seem to be going in slow motion as Turner put his finger on the trigger, but then his eyes got big just as he saw the gun aiming from a lower height than what he remembers previously. Seeing this puzzled Tyrone as he managed to get a shot off, but simultaneously, a shot came at him from other angles as a figure appeared from behind Tyrone and managed to get a shot off just before disappearing as quickly as it appeared. The guard was able to grab his gun from his leg holster to get a shot off in enough time to catch a leg of the unknown figure and tried to get another shot off at Tyrone as he found himself falling backwards with a least three gunshot wounds.

The courtroom erupted in chaos as the sound of gunshots echoed through the halls. The judge's decision hung in the balance, and the fate of all involved was thrown into uncertainty. As the dust settled, the shocking truth began to appear—for days and weeks to come.

LIVING THAT LIFE

Chapter 22:

The Aftermath of Plot

As a result of the actions made, Leroy and James were investigated for plotting a murder and hiring a shooter after the shooter confessed almost everything to the police. Due to only being out of prison for a short time, Leroy took full responsibility for his actions and asked that Glenn, Marcus, and James be cleared of any charges. The shooter, although shot, survived but continued to serve out his time, striking a plea deal that involved giving up his sources, which may have pointed directly to Leroy.

Terri found herself torn between relief and anguish. Tyrone, the man who had harmed her family, was dead, but the love of her life was once again bound by the chains of the legal system. Larissa was glad that L.J. had managed to keep his composure during the shooting and got her out of harm's way. She began to think about experiencing another shootout resulting with her own dad shooting at her. Terri noticed Larissa kind of looking down about everything that's going on. She decided to get them out of the house and took them to visit Leroy. She was sure that he needed comfort and support as he served whatever time he had. He told her that he was working on a plan with James.

One evening, as they relaxed watching television, Larissa suddenly blurted out, "Mommy, I killed Tyrone." Terri and L.J. exchanged a look of disbelief. L.J. started to speak, but Larissa quickly hushed him.

Terri, shaking her head in shock, told her children, "We will not speak of this again, do you hear me?" L.J. and Larissa nodded in agreement, but L.J. insisted they needed to talk to Leroy.

Two weeks later, Terri made an appointment to see Leroy. They sat down in front of him during visitation time, enjoying each other's company. Finally, Terri said, "Leroy, I have something to tell you, again." Leroy smiled, "I already know, honey." Terri looked at him, puzzled. "Know what?" Leroy leaned in, his voice low. "Do you remember the guy that tried to shoot Tyrone? The police are not stupid, Terri. They know where the angle the bullets came from."

Terri and the kids began to get nervous. Leroy calmed them down, explaining, "The shooter took a plea deal because he and I made a verbal deal. He agreed to take the fall for killing Tyrone and to say that I never offered him anything to do it. He owed me for protecting him just as I had done for Marcus in prison. L.J. gently interrupted, "But Dad, he didn't shoot Tyrone."

Leroy looked at his son, a mix of pride and concern in his eyes. "Son, this will be spoken about no more, okay?" They all agreed, promising never to speak of the incident again. Leroy asked them to keep the secret, explaining that his case would be dropped, and his record cleared if the truth about the shooting remained buried.

Three weeks later, Leroy was released. He took his family and invited friends and their families to church, marking the beginning of a new life without the shadows of the past looming over them. Or so they thought.

LIVING THAT LIFE

Chapter 23:

Shadows of the Past

Life seemed to return to normal for the family. Leroy Mathis stood in the doorway of his modest home, watching as his children, L.J. and Larissa, played in the yard. Their laughter filled the air, a sound that brought a smile to his face. He had secured a stable job at the warehouse, and though the work was hard, it provided for his family. Terri, his steadfast wife, stood by his side, her hand resting gently on his arm.

"Leroy, you did it, she said softly, her eyes reflecting the warmth of the setting sun. "You turned things around." Leroy nodded, a sense of pride and gratitude washing over him. "We did it, Terri. Together with the help of God." Across town, Glenn Williams stood at the pulpit of Temple Community Church, his voice resonating with conviction. The congregation listened intently, their hearts open to his message of forgiveness and redemption. The church had become a beacon of hope for the community, a place where people could find solace and support.

James struggles to walk without a cane every now and then but he's trying to make it to bible study each week. As he sat in the pews, his eyes closed in prayer. Thanks to the support of their family and the church community. He now worked as a youth counselor, helping others find their way off the streets and into a better life. He still struggles keeping his mind focused, and off the streets. James Street Smarts also knows it was too quiet for everything to go so smoothly.

Marcus and his girlfriend Yvonne sat nearby; their hands clasped tightly. Marcus had found a job at a local community center, using his experiences to mentor young men in the neighborhood. Yvonne, ever the supportive partner, continued to serve as an usher at the church, her warm smile welcoming everyone who entered. Marcus and James would meet up almost daily at the park playing basketball and keeping an eye on the streets while supporting their services for the youth at the church.

However, the shadow of the recent shootings still lingered over Temple, and the investigation brought them closer together. They were determined to build a brighter future for themselves and the children of the neighborhood. Glenn Williams would continue to lead his congregation with wisdom and compassion, delivering powerful sermons about forgiveness and redemption.

As the service ended, the congregation stood and sang a final hymn, their voices blending in harmony. Leroy looked around the sanctuary, his heart filled with gratitude. He had come a long way from his days in prison, and he knew that he owed it all to the love and support of his family and community. It seems like everything was back to normal.

Chapter 24:

The Morning Revelation

After watching the video footage again one morning as he sipped his coffee, Chief Swinson saw that although it looked like Larissa shot Tyrone, but as he looked again, he noticed something. The height of the gun lowered by about 5 inches just before the shots were fired. This discrepancy caught his attention, and he decided to investigate further.

Chief Swinson called his team into the conference room, the footage playing on the large screen. "Look at this," he said, pointing to the moment when the gun's height changed. "The gun is lowered lower just before the shots are fired. This doesn't add up."

The detectives leaned in, their eyes narrowing as they studied the footage. One of them spoke up, "Could it be that someone else was holding the gun?"

Chief Swinson nodded, his grave expression. "That's what we need to find out. We need to re-examine the crime scene and look for any bullet casings or bullet holes that match the trajectory of the shots fired. If we can find evidence that supports self-defense, it could change everything."

Chapter 25:

The Search for Truth

Chief Swinson and his team returned to the courthouse, their eyes scanning every inch of the crime scene. They measured the height of the bullet holes, comparing them to the footage. The discrepancy was clear—the bullet holes were lower than where Larissa would have been standing.

As they continued their search, they found a bullet casing lodged in the wall, matching the trajectory of the shots fired. Chief Swinson bagged the evidence, his mind racing with the implications. If Larissa had acted in self-defense, it would change the entire narrative of the case.

LIVING THAT LIFE

Chapter 26:

The Unsolved Issue

Back at the station, Chief Swinson and his team huddled around the evidence, their minds working overtime. The bullet casing and the height of the bullet holes pointed to self-defense, but there was still an unsolved issue. Why did the gun lower down in height just before the shooting took place?

Chief Swinson looked at his detectives, his voice firm. "We need to find out who was holding the gun. Was it L.J.? And if so, was it self-defense? We need to tread carefully here."

The detectives nodded, their expressions determined. They knew that the stakes were high, and they were prepared to leave no stone unturned in their quest for the truth.

LIVING THAT LIFE

Chapter 27:

The Family's Reaction

Meanwhile, Leroy and Terri were unaware of the new developments in the case. They continued to live their lives, focusing on their family and their future.

One evening, as they sat down to dinner, there was a knock at the door. Leroy opened it to find Chief Swinson and his detective standing on the other side. The chief's expression was grave, and Leroy knew that something was wrong.

"Leroy, Terri, we need to talk," Chief Swinson said, his voice firm. They invited him in, and he explained the situation, showing them the new evidence. Leroy and Terri listened intently, their hearts heavy with the weight of the revelation.

Terri's eyes filled with tears, and she looked at Leroy, her voice trembling. "What does this mean for our family?" she whispered. Leroy's face was pale, and he shook his head in disbelief. "We have to protect them," he said, his voice firm. "We can't let them go down for this."

Chapter 28:

The Community's Support

As the news of the new evidence spread throughout Temple, the community rallied behind Leroy and his family. This was not just about Leroy anymore. Now the kids are involved which makes this more dangerous for the Mathis family.

Pastor Glenn Williams played a crucial role in rallying the community. He delivered powerful sermons about forgiveness and redemption, reminding his congregation that everyone deserved a second chance. He also organized prayer vigils and support groups, offering solace and guidance to those in need.

Chapter 29:

The Truth Comes Out

As the investigation continued, the truth about the courthouse shooting began to appear. The media got wind of the story, and it quickly became a national sensation. Reporters descended onto Temple, eager to get the scoop on the shocking turn of events.

Leroy and Terri did their best to shield their children from the media frenzy, but they knew that it was only a matter of time before the truth came out. They braced themselves for the storm that was about to hit, vowing to stand together as a family no matter what.

Meanwhile, Chief Swinson and his team continued to follow every lead, determined to bring justice to the families affected by the violence. They knew that the truth would eventually come out, and they were prepared to face the consequences, no matter how difficult they might be.

Chapter 30:

A Family's Sacrifice

As the media frenzy reached its peak, Leroy and Terri made a difficult decision. They knew that they had to protect their family, no matter what the cost. They called a press conference and, with heavy hearts, confessed to their involvement in the plot to kill Tyrone.

Leroy explained that he had acted out of a desire to protect his family and that he took full responsibility for his actions. He also revealed that Larissa had been the one to pull the trigger, but he insisted that she had acted in self-defense.

The community was shocked by the revelation, but they also understood the depth of Leroy and Terri's love for their family. They rallied behind them, offering their support and prayers as they faced the difficult road ahead.

Chapter 31:

The Legal Battle

The confession set off a legal battle that would assess the limits of Leroy and Terri's resolve. They hired the best lawyers they could afford, determined to fight for their family's future. The prosecution, however, was relentless, and they were determined to see justice served.

As the trial unfolded, the courtroom was filled with tension. Witnesses took the stand, recounting the events of that fateful day. Leroy and Terri listened intently, their hearts heavy with the weight of their actions.

Meanwhile, Pastor Glenn Williams continued to rally the community, delivering powerful sermons about forgiveness and redemption. He also organized prayer vigils and support groups, offering solace and guidance to those in need.

Chapter 32:

New Hope

As the trial reached its climax, the jury deliberated for hours, weighing up the evidence and the testimonies. Finally, they reached a verdict, and the courtroom fell silent as the judge prepared to deliver the sentence.

To everyone's surprise, the jury found Leroy and Terri not guilty of the charges against them. The courtroom erupted in cheers, and Leroy and Terri embraced, their eyes filled with tears of relief and gratitude.

The community celebrated the verdict, and Pastor Glenn Williams delivered a powerful sermon about the power of forgiveness and redemption. He reminded his congregation that everyone deserved a second chance and that love, and compassion could overcome even the darkest of circumstances.

Chapter 33:

Family Reunited

With the legal battle behind them, Leroy and Terri focused on rebuilding their lives. They knew that the road ahead would be difficult, but they also knew that they had the love and support of their family and their community.

Leroy continued to work at the warehouse, and Terri devoted herself to her children and her involvement in the church. L.J. and Larissa, though forever changed by the events of that fateful day, found peace in their family's love and support.

Meanwhile, James has decided to keep a low profile until the full case is over and is relieved that the legal battle was over. But he has decided to get his life together once everything is back to normal.

Chapter 34:

The Looming Danger

As the days turned into weeks, the threat of retaliation grew more imminent. Tyrone's family and street crew were growing restless, and they were determined to seek revenge. They began to make their presence known throughout the community, their actions a clear warning of what was to come.

Leroy and Terri were on high alert, their eyes and ears open to any sign of danger. They knew that they had to be prepared for whatever might come their way, and they were determined to protect their family at all costs.

As the family and community of Temple began to heal and move forward, an unseen threat loomed on the horizon. Tyrone's family and street crew were not satisfied with the verdict. They believed that justice had not been served and were determined to seek revenge.

Rumors began to circulate throughout the community, whispers of retaliation and violence. Leroy and Terri were aware of the threat, but they were determined to protect their family at all costs. They knew that they had to be vigilant and prepared for whatever might come their way.

Leroy and Terri called a family meeting, and they explained the situation to L.J. and Larissa. The children were shocked and scared, but they understood the gravity of what was at stake. Leroy and Terri assured them that they would do everything in their power to protect them, and they vowed to stand together as a family.

As the rumors of retaliation continued to circulate, the community of Temple rallied behind Leroy and his family. They knew that the threat was real, and they were determined to stand together and protect one another.

LIVING THAT LIFE

Chapter 35:

New Charges Filed

In the days that followed, the police investigated the shooting, piecing together the events that led to Tyrone's death. Leroy, though initially suspected of hiring the shooter, was cleared of all charges. The focus shifted to Larissa and L.J., who had been at the center of chaos. The court met to figure out who had pulled the trigger and if it was in self-defense.

Larissa, her small hands trembling, couldn't have fired the gun. The court ruled that she was incapable of pulling the trigger, shifting the spotlight to L.J. But L.J. was nowhere to be found. He had fled the courthouse, disappearing into the streets of Temple, leaving behind a family in turmoil and a community on edge.

L.J. found himself at James's house, a place he thought would be safe from the prying eyes of the law. James, his uncle, had always been a figure of strength and wisdom in his life. As he sat in the dimly lit living room, L.J. couldn't help but feel a mix of relief and fear.

"L.J., you can't stay here forever. The police are looking for you, and it's only a matter of time before they start knocking on doors.", James said.

L.J. looked up at his uncle, his eyes filled with desperation. "I didn't know what else to do, Uncle

James. I panicked. I couldn't face the court, not after everything that happened."

James sighed, sitting down beside his nephew. "I understand, L.J. But running away isn't the answer. You need to face the consequences of your actions. The truth will come out eventually."

L.J. shook his head, his voice barely above a whisper. "But what if they don't believe me? What if they think I did it on purpose? It was all a mistake."

James placed a reassuring hand on L.J.'s shoulder. "You have to trust in the justice system, L.J. They will see the truth. But you must give them a chance. You can't hide forever."

L.J. looked down at his hands, remembering the weight of the gun and the chaos of that fateful day. "I was so scared, Uncle James. I saw Tyrone pointing at Larissa, and I just reacted. I didn't think about the consequences. I just wanted to protect her."

James nodded; his expression thoughtful. "I know, L.J. And I believe you. But you must tell your story to the court. They need to hear your side of what happened. Running away only makes you look guilty."

L.J. took a deep breath, his mind racing with thoughts of what lay ahead. "What if they don't believe me? What if I go to jail?"

James looked at his nephew, his voice firm but gentle. "You have to have faith, L.J. The truth will set you free. But you have to be brave and face the music. Hiding here won't change what happened. It's time to do the right thing."

L.J. knew his uncle was right. He couldn't run forever. He had to face the consequences of his actions and trust that the justice system would see the truth. With a heavy heart, he made his decision.

LJ began saying, "Okay, Uncle James. I'll turn myself in. I'll tell them everything that happened. I just hope they believe me."

James smiled, a sense of pride and relief washing over him. "That's the right thing to do, L.J. I'll go with you to the police station. We'll face this together."

As they prepared to leave, L.J. felt a sense of resolve. He knew the road ahead would be difficult, but he also knew that facing the truth was the only way to find peace. With his uncle by his side, he was ready to step out into the world and confront the consequences of his actions. But James had a thought and said, "Wait a minute LJ, let me go do my own investigation to see if it is safe for you to come forth with your side of the story. Wait, here a little longer, I'll be back. Don't leave. LJ said, okay Uncle James, I'll be here.

LIVING THAT LIFE

Chapter 36:

The Discovery

Chief Swinson sat in his office, the weight of the courthouse shooting heavy on his shoulders. The city was on edge, and Tyrone Turner's family and street crew grew restless, demanding answers. The detective assigned to the case had been meticulous, combing through every piece of evidence, every witness statement. But it was the security camera footage that held the key.

The detective burst into Chief Swinson's office, a USB drive in hand. "Chief, we found something. The security camera in the courthouse lobby captured the entire shooting."

Chief Swinson's eyes widened. "Let's see it."

They plugged the USB drive into the computer, and the grainy footage began to play. The courthouse lobby was filled with a couple of people as the camera was focused on the entrance. Suddenly, chaos erupted. Shots rang out, and people scattered. The camera zoomed in on Tyrone Turner, who was standing near the courtroom side door.

The footage showed a figure in some kind of hoodie or loose-fitting cap, face obscured, firing the first shot. A security officer fell to the ground, but the shooting didn't stop. The second Security officer with his gun drawn shooting back at the first shooter, then down goes an inmate, but Tyrone still standing but he now has the fallen security officer's gun.   More shots were displayed.

The forensic team worked tirelessly, analyzing the bullets retrieved from Tyrone's body and the courthouse lobby. The results were shocking. It appears to be 5 different guns had been used in the shooting. One belonged to the hooded figure, and the other one may match the gun drawn by L.J. Mathis.

Chapter 37:

The 3rd Shooter

Chief Swinson called a meeting with his top detectives. "We have a problem. The forensic report shows that one of the bullets that hit Tyrone may have come from Officer Johnson's gun. Johnson was standing a little bit behind Tyrone, a bullet found had entered from the back.

The room fell silent. Officer Johnson is a respected member of the force, known for his dedication and integrity. But the evidence was clear.

"We need to bring him in for questioning," Chief Swinson said. "And we need to find out which bullet ended Tyrone's life. Tyrone's family and crew are getting impatient. We can't let them take matters into their own hands."

Chapter 38:

The Interrogation

Officer Johnson sat in the interrogation room; his face puzzled. Chief Swinson and the detective entered; their expressions were grim.

"Officer Johnson, we need to talk about the courthouse shooting," Chief Swinson began.

Johnson looked up; his eyes filled with fear. "I didn't mean to shoot him, Chief. It was an accident. I was aiming for the shooter, but evidently Tyrone must've gotten in the way."

The detective leaned forward. "What do you mean must've gotten in the way? You should know, you were there! We need the truth, Johnson. The forensic report doesn't lie." Johnson took a deep breath saying, "I am telling the truth! I panicked. I saw the shooter, and I fired. I didn't realize Tyrone was in the line of fire until it was too late." Chief Swinson nodded. "We'll need your full statement. And we'll need to suspend you pending further investigation." Johnson hung his head, defeated. "I understand, Chief."

Chapter 39:

The Hooded Figure

The detective worked tirelessly, poring over the security footage and witness statements. He finally got a break when a witness came forward, naming the hooded figure as James, a known associate of Leroy. James? "I thought we had the hooded figure," Chief Swinson replied. Chief, the hired shooter, was an inmate, no hoodie, He covered his head with a towel. It looked like a hoodie, said Officer Tisdale. Chief replied, "This is a big mess! We have two new so-called leaders named Darrell Harper and Mike Whitherspoon, a little juvenile suspect on the run, and a 3rd shooter on the loose. Tisdale, I am turning this case over to you, I do not like the way this is looking. Call Officer Johnson back in.

Tisdale and Swinson view multiple footage and saw a flash coming from behind Officer Johnson around the same time that Tyrone and L.J. guns discharged. "That's why this case seemed to be so hard", Swinson said. Tisdale replied, "What do you see Chief"? Chief Said, "I knew I had a reason to call Johnson back in. Where is he, is he here yet?". "He's walking in now Chief", Tisdale replied.

The Chief began to question Johnson again. "Johnson, you told us that you were trying to shoot the shooter." Yes, that's correct Chief", Johnson replied. Chief goes on to ask, "How many shooters did you see'? "Johnson hesitates, then says, I don't recall". Chief starts to get frustrated from the vague responses that he's getting from Johnson. "Why aren't you talking Johnson", yelled Chief. Tisdale steps in saying, "Chief. What is it Tisdale! Chief asked. "Do you mind if I talk with Johnson"? Tisdale replied. "Sure, maybe he'll say something"! Chief proclaimed. Tisdale began to speak, "Okay Johnson, we need your help, and you know this. We know that there are at least three shooters. But we think there are five different guns involved. Can you explain all of this to us since you were there? Wait a minute before you start. Did you see this man, James Williams there? Now you may speak.

Johnson first shows Tisdale a note. Tisdale asked, "what is this"? Johnson responded by saying that someone walked up to me and handed me the little note with my name and address on it along with the name of my kid's schools. It also said for me to keep my mouth shut. That's one reason why I couldn't say anything. "What's the other reason?" Chief Swinson asked. I couldn't see who it was. So, when I said that I was shooting at the shooter, he is the shooter that I shot at. I think I shot him in his leg or at least grazed his leg. He's probably walking around limping.

Okay troops, I am in charge now and we're doing this my way, ordered Tisdale. He ordered a raid on James's hideout. The SWAT team moved in; weapons were drawn. But they were caught off guard when they were surprised by a room of people praying. James was standing next to Marcus waiting for them whenever they came for him. James did not go down fighting. He just smiled and put his hands behind his back and waited. He had just given his life to God. During the prayer he confessed his sins including the shooting. He was apprehended at once by Officer Tisdale.

Back at the station in the interrogation room, James changed his statement after hearing about 2 other shooters and sneered at the detective. "You got nothing on me."

The detective slammed a photo of Tyrone on the table. "We have you on camera, James. You shot Tyrone; they said you confessed to the shooting during prayer. Why?" Why change your statement now?

Jame's said," Number one, you can't even see the face of the shooter on this photo and if I wanted to shoot him, there are plenty of reasons that anybody would've wanted Tyrone dead. "He was a threat. He was taking over our neighborhood and he has to stop hurting people just for the fun of it."

But like I said, I am not your guy. Chief Swinson entered the room saying," I have heard enough! You're under arrest for the murder of Tyrone Turner. And we have enough evidence to put you away for a long time."

Chapter 40:

The Family's Reaction

News of the arrests spread quickly. James's family were outraged. They gathered at Pastor Glenn Williams's church, demanding justice.

Pastor Williams stood before the congregation, his voice steady. "We must trust in the justice system. Violence will not bring Tyrone or Wesley back to their family, neither will hurting or killing get James and LJ freed, we pray that L.J gets found alive before we're burying a family member. We must pray for peace and let the law take its course."

But Leroy was not convinced by saying, "We can't just sit here and do nothing. We need to defend ourselves. The police are supposed to help us. They won't stop until they have taken everything from us. I've been arrested, my son is still missing and there is already someone in jail for the shooting. But that's not enough for them! Now they're trying to take down James too, who else is next?

Marcus nodded in agreement. "We need to strap up. We can't let them get away with this." Pastor Williams looked at them, his eyes filled with sadness. "Violence begets violence. We must find another way."

Leroy, Terrence, and Marcus huddled in a corner of the church; their voices low. "We can't just sit here and wait for them to come for us," Leroy said.

Terrence nodded. "We need to be ready. We need to defend ourselves."

Marcus looked at them, his expression determined. "We'll do whatever it takes to protect our family and our territory."

Pastor Williams watched them from a distance, his heart heavy. He knew the path they were choosing was dangerous, but he also knew the strength of their loyalty to each other. He prayed silently, hoping for a miracle.

LIVING THAT LIFE

Chapter 41:

The Confrontation

The streets were tense as Leroy, Terrence, and Marcus patrolled their territory; weapons hidden but ready. They knew that the crew would retaliate, and they were prepared.

One night, as they walked down a dark alley by the neighborhood park, they heard footsteps behind them. They turned to see Darrell Harper, the crew's leader with guns drawn.

Marcus stepped forward; his voice was steady. "You want a war? We'll give you a war." The air was thick with tension, but before any shots could be fired, sirens blared in the distance. Police cars screeched to a halt, and officers poured out, weapons drawn, Chief Swinson stepped forward, his firm; "drop your weapons. This ends now." Leroy and Marcus exchanged glances, then slowly backed back. The police moved in, Darrell and his crew escaped to avoid capture.

Chief Swinson looked at Darrell yelling, "Son, I don't know you, but this is not what you want to do. Violence is not the answer"!

Then he turned to Leroy saying, "Leroy, things aren't looking too good. There is another member of your family that took part in the courthouse shooting and I got a feeling you already know this. I don't know what you're thinking, but you need to listen to your brother-in-law Williams, and even he's not innocent himself. Tisdale pulls Leroy to the side.

"What, what do you mean"? Leroy replied. How do you know when to be at the house that Tyrone burglarized 12 years ago? He should've done his full time just like you and Marcus did. And do you really think that I didn't see him in that car, your getaway car? Tisdale grinning. We needed somebody on the outside to keep us informed. Leroy began saying, "so Glenn's a snitch"? Tisdale walks back to his vehicle saying, Leroy, think about it, how else would we know your whereabouts tonight? "I'll be checking on y'all from time to time. Just to let you know, we have an eyewitness placing James at the courthouse, we have an officer who claims that he shot James in the leg, and when we brought James in for questioning, he was limping". I just thought you should know.

All the police left leaving Leroy, Marcus and Terrence standing there with puzzled expressions on their faces.

Marcus asked Leroy, "What was that all about"? Leroy responded, they know just as much as we do. Unfortunately, I know how. As he lowers his head in shame.

Chapter 42:

Street Showdown

Days later, after hearing that James was released for lack of evidence. The new leader Darrell, vows to honor Tyrone's legacy and is determined to kill anyone that had any part in Tyrone's or Wesley's death. This included any members associated with their crew. He was targeting Leroy, James, Glenn or even L.J. They heard that LJ may have been Tyrone's killer and that he is on the run. The tension in Temple reached a boiling point. Darrell and his crew were determined to seek revenge, and they made their move.

James called a meeting to meet with Leroy to let him know his whereabouts. He agreed to pick him up. As he drives, he begins thinking of the plans that they previously came up with. After he arrives, James gets in the car. Leroy asked, "Hey James, how did Tisdale find out about our plans man"? James answered, "Man, I don't even know, almost caught me off guard. I had begun to confess too, at least until I realized that the evidence that they had couldn't prove anything. "So, they had to let you go, Leroy added", James giggles saying, "That's right"! Leroy began to tell James what Tisdale told him concerning Glenn. Did you know that Glenn had been an informant for the police? And they know that Glenn took part in that burglary. They've been twisting his arms for years. That's how he became a leader in our community and was able to get everyone to work together. James said, "but that's a good thing though, right?" Leroy responded, umm, yes, I guess.

They went on and picked up Terrence and Marcus. Terrence mentioned, I just got a call about a shooting, I think my dad is supposed to have a peaceful meeting today. They said during the meeting, there was a shootout taking place not too far from where they hung out at. James asked, "Is this it? Should we head over there". Marcus answered, "Well, we've met previously about this day already, maybe this is it". Terrence asked, "What if my dad is over there, he didn't return my call. He was meeting there for a peaceful demonstration". "Awe man, that's right, Leroy said. Glenn was supposed to protest by the park today and we were supposed to be there too. So, I guess we need to head over there. James yelled out, go back by my house first, we need to be ready.

They made their way up the street to see who they could help get out of harm's way. These were innocent people that were being targeted. Leroy spoke saying, "okay, let the police have this fight while we get these people to safety, if we can. Lord helps us get out of this mess please! Leroy prayed".

A violent shootout erupted between the police and Darrell's gang, with protesters caught in the crossfire. The streets echoed with the sound of gunshots, and the air was thick with the scent of gunpowder.

As the shootout intensified, more injuries were reported, and the community of Temple held its breath, waiting for the storm to pass. Just as the situation seemed to spiral out of control, a figure appeared from the shadows. Officer Tisdale pulled out his mega horn and beamed bright lights towards the figure that's standing there is mist of turmoil and yells, "cease fire". Everyone listens for a moment. While the police attention was on the unknown figure, Darrell gathered up his crew and took off as fast as they could, which Leroy gets a closer look and yells out, LJ! They ran towards each other with a mixture of excitement and sorrow. Tisdale allows them to enjoy each other's company for a few minutes before taking L.J into custody for murder. Tisdale radioed Chief Swinson, "Hey Chief, we did have a little gun play, but it seems to be only minor injuries. But we know who they are. L.J showed up right in the mist of the shooting, can you believe that? I'm going to see if he'll take me the gun that he ditched. We've already called for medical aid. Chief said jokingly, "It looks like I missed all the fun today.

Chapter 43:

The Murder Weapon

Officer Tisdale ask L.J, "Can you take us to where you ditched the gun that you had?" LJ lowered his head and said, "If I could ride with my dad, yes, I'll show you. Tisdale granted the wish and followed them to the destination.

The police retrieved the gun from its hiding place, and L.J. was taken into custody, his fate hanging in the balance. The community of Temple rallied behind him, determined to prove his innocence and fight for his freedom. Peaceful protests echoed through the streets, a testament to the unity and strength of a community under siege.

L.J. revealed the truth: Larissa and I had a plan to be in place the kill Tyrone just in case the hired shooter missed. So when I saw the first two shots had missed Tyrone and hit the security officer in front and one of the inmates had gotten hit too, I guess I panicked when I saw Tyrone still standing and grabbing the security officers gun and shot back at the hired shooter who had started running away as he was still shooting at Tyrone, but then it looked like Tyrone was starring right at me and I froze up and dropped the gun. But there was a security officer coming up from behind Tyrone aiming and shooting down the hall at gunman running away, but then Tyrone started to turn around toward the security guard but stopped in mid motion with a smirk on his face looking back at me, at least that's what I thought, but then I realized as I looked down at Larissa that he was glazing at her. She had this look on her face as she tried to pull the trigger, but she couldn't pull it. I looked back at Tyrone and saw his finger moving towards the trigger and before I knew it, I grabbed Larissa pulling her back and downward as I grabbed the gun from her keeping it pointed towards Tyrone. Once Larissa was all the way down, she used her legs to push me to help me to keep my balance as I held the gun with both hands. It was as if everything was going in slow motion as we shot at each other simultaneously, but it seemed like bullets flew in from everywhere. But two of the shots came from behind Tyrone. But as I looked, I didn't see anything. So, then I got up and grabbed Larissa and the gun and we ran out to the side where we had come in to ditch the gun. That's everything that I know. Tyrone was going to shoot Larissa again, and I couldn't go through that again. We came back in and tried blending in with the crowd as chaos erupted.

Chapter 44:

The Verdict Awaits

The courtroom was packed to capacity, every seat filled with anxious residents of Temple. The air was thick with anticipation as Judge Martha Henderson entered, her stern gaze sweeping over the crowd. L.J. sat at the defendant's table, his eyes fixed straight ahead, a mixture of fear and determination etched on his young face.

The prosecution had painted a grim picture, portraying L.J. as a vengeful teenager who had acted out of malice rather than self-defense. They argued that his actions at the courthouse were premeditated, a cold-blooded response to Tyrone's provocations. The defense, however, presented a different narrative. They highlighted L.J.'s desperate attempt to protect Larissa, his split-second decision to grab the gun, and the chaos that ensued.

Witnesses were called to the stand, each offering a piece of the puzzle. Larissa testified, her voice trembling as she recounted the terror of that day. She described how L.J. had her, his actions driven by instinct and fear rather than revenge. Darrell's crew members, surprisingly, also took the stand, their testimonies conflicting but ultimately revealing the deep-seated tensions that had led to the shootout.

As the trial ended, Judge Henderson called for a recess. The courtroom buzzed with speculation, whispers of what the verdict might be. L.J.'s fate hung in the balance, and the community of Temple held its breath, waiting for the decision that would shape their future.

Outside the courthouse, the streets were filled with protesters, their signs and chants echoing the sentiment of unity and justice. The peaceful demonstrations were a stark contrast to the violence that had once plagued Temple. The community had rallied behind L.J., determined to see justice served.

As the court reconvened, Judge Henderson's expression was unreadable. She shuffled her papers, the silence in the courtroom deafening. Finally, she spoke, her voice clear and measured.

"The decision before us is not an easy one," she began. "The events that transpired at the courthouse were tragic and complex. The actions of L.J. must be examined through the lens of self-defense and the circumstances that led to his decisions."

She paused, her gaze resting on L.J. "The court has considered all the evidence presented, the testimonies of the witnesses, and the arguments of both the prosecution and the defense. L.J.'s actions were not driven by malice but by a desire to protect those he cared for."

A murmur rippled through the courtroom, hope flickering in the eyes of those present. However, Judge Henderson continued, "the law must be upheld, and the consequences of one's actions must be addressed. The court will consider L.J.'s age and the extraordinary circumstances surrounding the incident."

She took a deep breath, her next words hanging in the air. "The court will reconvene in one week to deliver the final verdict. Until then, L.J. will remain in custody."

The courtroom erupted in a mix of relief and anxiety. L.J.'s fate was still uncertain, but the community of Temple knew that their fight for justice was far from over. As the days passed, they would stand united, awaiting the verdict that would figure out not just L.J.'s future, but the future of their community. The verdict awaited, and with it, the promise of a new beginning or the echo of a past that refused to be silenced.

Chapter 45:

The Unthinkable Verdict

Two weeks had passed like a slow-burning fuse, each day ticking closer to the moment of truth. The community of Temple had rallied tirelessly, their voices echoing through the streets, demanding justice and fairness. The courthouse was once again filled to the brim, the air thick with a palpable tension that seemed to hum with the collective heartbeat of those present.

Judge Martha Henderson entered the courtroom, her expression grave. L.J. stood, his hands clasped tightly in front of him, his eyes fixed on the judge. The room fell silent, the only sound the faint rustle of papers as the judge prepared to deliver her verdict.

"The court has carefully considered all the evidence, the testimonies, and the arguments presented," Judge Henderson began, her voice steady and measured. "The decision before us is one of great consequences, not just for L.J., but for the community of Temple as a whole."

She paused, her gaze sweeping over the courtroom before settling back on L.J. "The court finds that L.J.'s actions, while driven by a desire to protect, were nonetheless reckless and endangered the lives of others. Therefore, L.J. will be tried as an adult and will face charges of manslaughter."

A collective gasp rippled through the courtroom, followed by a wave of shocked murmurs. L.J.'s eyes widened in disbelief, his body swaying slightly as if the weight of the verdict had physically struck him. Larissa, seated in the front row, let out a soft cry, her hands flying to her mouth.

Judge Henderson raised her hand, calling for order. "However," she continued, her voice cutting through the noise, "the court also recognizes the extraordinary circumstances surrounding the incident. L.J.'s actions were not premeditated, and he acted under extreme duress. Therefore, the court will recommend a reduced sentence, taking into account his age and the mitigating factors."

The courtroom erupted into chaos. Some shouted outrage, others in relief, but all were united in their shock. The verdict was a double-edged sword, acknowledging L.J.'s intent while still holding him accountable for his actions.

As the court adjourned, L.J. was led away, his eyes haunted but resolute. The community of Temple, stunned by the verdict, began to mobilize. Protests erupted anew, this time with fiercer determination. The fight for L.J.'s freedom had only just begun.

Chapter 46:

A New Dawn of Resistance

In the days that followed, Temple became a hotbed of activism. The community, galvanized by the verdict, refused to accept it as the final word. Legal experts were consulted, petitions were signed, and rallies were organized. The streets echoed with chants of "Justice for L.J.," a battle cry that resonated through every corner of the city.

Larissa, now a symbol of the community's resilience, stood at the forefront of the movement. She spoke at rallies, her voice strong and unyielding, recounting the events of that fateful day and the injustice of the verdict. Darrell, surprisingly happy about the court's decision, also lent his support, his crew joining the protests in a show of unity that would have been unthinkable just weeks ago. Of course, all they did was sat around in small groups taunting LJ's supporters.

Meanwhile, L.J., confined to a cell, found peace in the letters and messages of support that poured in. He wrote back; his words filled with gratitude and a renewed determination to fight for his freedom. His lawyers worked tirelessly, preparing for the appeal that would challenge the verdict and look for a more just outcome.

As the days turned into weeks, the fight for L.J.'s freedom became more than just a legal battle. It has become a symbol of the community's struggle against injustice.

The verdict had been made, but the fight was far from over. The community stood united, ready to face whatever challenges lay ahead, their voices echoing through the streets, demanding justice, demanding change.

Chapter 47:

A Father's Wisdom

The visiting room of the county jail was a stark, cold place, the air heavy with the weight of countless conversations filled with longing, regret, and hope. L.J. sat at a small table, his hands folded in front of him, his eyes fixed on the door. When it finally opened, and Leroy Mathis stepped in, L.J.'s face lit up with a mixture of relief and apprehension.

Leroy, a tall, broad-shouldered man with a face etched by time and hardship, walked over to the table and sat down across from his son. His eyes, mirrors of L.J.'s own, held a depth of understanding that only experience could bring. For a moment, they just looked at each other, the silence between them speaking volumes.

"Hey, son," Leroy finally said, his voice gruff with emotion. "Hey, Dad," L.J. replied, his voice barely above a whisper. Leroy leaned back in his chair, his gaze never leaving L.J.'s face. "I know this isn't easy, L.J. I know exactly how you feel." L.J. nodded, his eyes welling up. "I'm scared, Dad. I don't know what's going to happen." Leroy reached across the table, his large hand covering L.J.'s. "I know, son. I know. But you have stay strong and you have to keep fighting". L.J. took a deep breath, trying to steady himself. "What was it like for you when you were here?"

Leroy's expression grew distant, his mind traveling back to the years he had spent behind bars. "It was tough, L.J. Real tough. But I learned a lot. I learned about patience and resilience. I learned that no matter how dark things get, there's always a way out."

He leaned forward, his voice dropping to a low, intense whisper. "You have to keep your head up, son. You just stay focused on the appeal. Your lawyers are working hard, and the community is behind you. You're not alone in this fight."

L.J. nodded, his grip on his father's hand tightening. " I just don't want to let anyone down. I don't want to let you down."

Leroy's eyes softened, and he shook his head. "You could never let me down. You hear me? Never. You're my son, and I'm proud of you. No matter what happens, I'm proud of you."

L.J.'s eyes filled with tears, and he quickly wiped them away. "Thanks, Dad. That means a lot."

Leroy nodded, his own eyes glistening. "Now, listen. You got to be smart here. Keep your head down, stay out of trouble. Use this time to think, to plan. When you get out—and you will get out—you must be ready to have an influence. You have to be ready to help this community heal." L.J. took a deep breath, his father's words sinking in. "I will, Dad. I promise." Leroy smiled, a rare, genuine smile that lit up his face. "That's my boy.

As the visiting time ended, Leroy stood up, his hand resting on L.J.'s shoulder. "Remember son. You're not alone. You've got a whole community behind you, and you've got me. We're going to get through this together."

L.J. nodded, his eyes filled with a newfound resolve. "Together, Dad. We'll get through this together." As Leroy got up, he said, "Hey son, there's one more person that's been waiting in the waiting room wanting to see you, as he walked away. L.J said who as he watched his dad smile while walking out with his heart filled with a mixture of love, gratitude, and determination.

LIVING THAT LIFE

Chapter 48:

The New Plan

James entered the room with a confident stride, greeting his nephew warmly. "Hey, nephew!" he said, a smile playing on his lips.

L.J. looked up, a mix of curiosity and anticipation in his eyes. "Uncle James, how are you doing?" he asked, his voice steady but tinged with a hint of nervousness.

"I'm fine," James replied, his tone reassuring. "Listen, nephew, thanks for covering for me at the courthouse. Visitation time is almost over, so pay attention."

L.J. leaned in, his focus unwavering as James began to lay out the rest of the plan. "As you know, nobody knows that this plan involves your dad and Larissa too, and we're going to keep it that way. Everyone played their part, so all that's left is for you to play yours."

James paused, a smirk crossing his face. "I already took care of the switch while everyone was out looking for you. I have to say, both of us disappearing at the same time was brilliant."

L.J. nodded, a sense of pride swelling within him. "Yes, it was. And thanks for letting me hide at your place."

"No problem, nephew," James said, his voice softening. "I almost didn't get off until I realized that they figured out there were at least two shooters and no clear visual on me. But now we're back on track."

James's expression turned serious as he continued. "Like I said, I switched the guns. I went and got the gun that you and Larissa had and replaced it with mine. They're going to wreck their brains trying to figure out how you shot Tyrone in the back from the angle you were in."

He leaned in closer, his voice dropping to a whisper. "You see, the gun that they have is the one I had both of you practicing with prior to going to court. So, it has both of your fingerprints on it. I use gloves, so my prints won't show up. I cleaned the gun that you used."

L.J.'s eyes widened as the gravity of James's words sank in. "You do know that your shot is most likely going to be the bullet that ended Tyrone's life. It was the closest shot to his heart."

James nodded, his gaze steady. "Remember the gun that they have in evidence? It's the one I shot him with, but it hit him on the shoulder blade. So, the third bullet that they found in Tyrone will come up as the lethal shot instead of yours."

He took a deep breath, his mind racing with the intricate details of the plan. "But we both know your dad took care of everything by putting together the plea deal that the police made with the inmate that your dad hired. That deal excluded your dad from taking any part of the plan that hired him. So, they already have the man they're looking for."

A smirk played on James's lips as he imagined the scene. "I just want to see his face when they tell him that he killed Tyrone. That plea deal is going right out of the window."

As James finished speaking, L.J. sat there, absorbing every word, his mind a whirlwind of thoughts and emotions. The plan was complex, meticulously crafted, and carried out with precision. He knew that the road ahead was uncertain, but with his father's wisdom, his uncle's street knowledge, and the community's support, he was ready to face whatever challenges lay ahead. The fight for his freedom was far from over, but he was determined to see it through to the end.

LIVING THAT LIFE

Chapter 49:

The Unknown Pressure

Days later, Chief Swinson's phone rang incessantly. First, it was forensics, then the coroner's office, and finally, the District Attorney's office. Each call carried the same ominous message: "We have a big problem. Nothing is matching up. What's going on?"

Chief Swinson's voice boomed through the office, "Tisdale!"

Tisdale rushed in; concern etched on his face. "What is it, Chief?"

Chief Swinson rubbed his temples. "Apparently, the kid didn't fire the fatal shot. That leaves a host of other explanations, including either the unidentified guy or the inmate who may be the hired killer."

Tisdale's eyes widened while saying, "so, this case involves five guns, nine bullet casings, five shooters, and six bullets embedded within 3 bodies, with four of the six bullets in one body. And through all of that, we must find out which shooter shot the fatal bullet into Tyrone Turner?"

Chief Swinson looked at Tisdale with a puzzled expression. "Yes, you're correct. Tisdale, we've been played by James Williams! Somehow, we'll get him, but for now let's review each shooter versus each gun."

Swinson began, "According to the camera, the hired inmate shot first, most likely hitting the security officer standing in front of the inmates. He also fired the second shot, which hit an inmate."

Tisdale nodded. "So, before he could shoot again, Tyrone had taken the guard's gun and shot at the shooter, causing him to start running away. That's three shots right there. Everything happened so fast around the same time."

Swinson agreed. " Yes sir. It looks like as if the shooter turned to shoot again, Tyrone glanced downward to his right as he pointed his gun towards the kids. This is getting even more interesting. By looking at these other camera angles we found, L.J. shot Tyrone just as Tyrone shot his gun at L.J., but Tyrone missed the kid because he was getting shot again from the front angle by the hired gunman, who also dodged the bullet we found in the wall from the security officers standing in the rear."

Tisdale, check this out," the Chief continued. "As that same officer shot his gun at the original gunman, a bullet passed by him and hit Tyrone in the back, causing that officer to turn around to shoot at the unknown shooter hiding in the shadows. I don't know how we are going to explain all of this in court. Tisdale, I just don't know.

Tisdale began, "You say two in custody for three murders and one unknown wounded, and we already know who that is, Mr. James played us big time. He knew those cameras were old. But at least we have at least one person in custody."

Swinson interrupted; "Tisdale, we have two in custody."

Tisdale responded, "Chief, we only have evidence on one person now."

"We can no longer hold L.J. for murder or even try him again unless we give him lesser charges and try him as a juvenile."

Chief Swinson and Tisdale looked at each other, as Chief said, "I guess you better tell that inmate that he may be taking the fall for Tyrone's death without the plea bargain."

Tisdale looked down, knowing that he was the one who convinced the inmate to take the deal in the first place. The inmate had only taken it for the possibility of being released early or at least after ten years. Now he might be looking at life, especially since they could see that he shot a third time, hitting Tyrone in the chest, which might end up being the fatal shot instead of L.J.'s bullet. This meant they had been holding the killer in jail the whole time, with cameras showing that he killed all three men.

Chief Swinson, with a caring voice, said, "You knew what this job entailed when you accepted it in the beginning. If the situation bothers you, prove that James was a shooter, at least for manslaughter, and L.J. should go to juvenile if the murder charge as an adult doesn't stick. It's continuous work, Tisdale!" They glanced at each other with a nod before leaving the room…

Chapter 50:

Unraveling the Truth

The courthouse was abuzz with activity as the investigation into the murder of Tyrone Turner, the security officer, and the inmate continued. Chief Swinson and Tisdale were at the forefront, determined to uncover the truth.

In the interrogation room, the hired inmate sat, his eyes darting nervously. Chief Swinson leaned in, his voice stern. "We know you shot first. We have it all on camera. But what we need to know is why."

The inmate swallowed hard. "I was paid to take out Tyrone. I didn't know about the others. It was supposed to be a clean job."

Tisdale, standing in the corner, shook his head. "Nothing about this was clean. Three people are dead, and you're looking at life behind bars."

Meanwhile, in another room, L.J. sat with his lawyer, his young face etched with fear. "I didn't mean to kill anyone. I was just trying to protect myself."

His lawyer patted his shoulder. "We'll fight to have you tried as a juvenile. You're just a kid, L.J. The system should recognize that."

Chapter 51:

The Trial Begins

The courtroom was packed as the trial of the hired inmate began. The prosecution presented their case, showing the jury the footage from the courthouse cameras. The inmate's shots were clear, and the gasps from the jury echoed through the room.

The defense argued that the inmate was coerced, that he had no choice but to follow orders. But the prosecution was relentless. "He had a choice," they argued. "And he made the wrong one."

In a separate courtroom, L.J.'s trial was also underway. The prosecution pushed him to be tried as an adult, citing the severity of his actions. But L.J.'s lawyer fought back, presenting L.J. as a scared kid who made a terrible mistake.

LIVING THAT LIFE

Chapter 52:

The Verdict

The jury deliberated for days in the inmate's trial. Finally, they reached a verdict. Guilty on all counts. The inmate was sentenced to life in prison without the possibility of parole.

In L.J.'s trial, the jury also reached a verdict. They found him guilty of manslaughter but agreed that he should be tried as a juvenile. The judge sentenced him to a juvenile detention facility until he turned 18.

LIVING THAT LIFE

Chapter 53:

Moving Forward

As the trials concluded, Chief Swinson and Tisdale reflected on the cases. "We did our best," Tisdale said, sighing. "But it's never easy."

Chief Swinson nodded. "No, it's not. But we got justice for Tyrone, the security officer, and the inmate. And L.J. has a chance to turn his life around."

The courthouse murders had shaken the community, but the investigations and trials brought a sense of closure. The truth had been uncovered, and justice had been served.

LIVING THAT LIFE

Chapter 54:

The Search for Answers

The precinct was alive with tension as Chief Swinson and Tisdale pored over the evidence once again. They weren't satisfied. There were still too many unanswered questions, too many loose ends.

"We need more on James," Chief Swinson said, his voice firm. "I want to know exactly what his involvement was in Tyrone's murder."

Tisdale nodded, his eyes scanning the reports in front of him. "And what about the second security officer? There's still a chance he participated in the shooting of Tyrone and James."

Chief Swinson leaned back in his chair, his mind racing. "We need to find that blood trail. If James was shot in the courthouse hallway, there has to be evidence."

LIVING THAT LIFE

Chapter 55:

The Blood Trail

The courthouse was eerily quiet as the forensic team combed through the hallway, their flashlights casting long shadows. Tisdale knelt, his gloved hand pointing to a small, dark stain on the floor.

"Here," he called out. "This is it. The blood trail starts here."

Chief Swinson joined him, his eyes following the trail down the hallway. "Good work, Tisdale. Let's get this analyzed. If it's James's blood, we'll have our evidence."

Chapter 56:

The Court Order

The courtroom was packed as James limped to the stand. The judge's voice echoed through the room.

"Mr. James, the court orders you to explain why you are limping. We have reason to believe it is related to the courthouse shooting."

James swallowed hard, his hands trembling. "I was shot that day, Your Honor. I didn't want to get involved, but I had no choice."

The prosecutor stood up; his voice sharp. "And why did you have no choice, Mr. James? Were you involved in Tyrone's murder?"

James hesitated, his eyes darting around the room. "I... I was there. But I didn't pull the trigger. I swear."

LIVING THAT LIFE

Chapter 57:

The Truth Unfolds

Back at the precinct, Chief Swinson and Tisdale reviewed the new evidence. The blood trail was indeed James's, and the forensic report confirmed it.

"We've got him," Tisdale said, a sense of satisfaction in his voice. "James was involved. We just need to find out how deep it goes."

Chief Swinson nodded, his mind already racing ahead. "We're not done yet, Tisdale. We need to find out if Officer Johnson is willing to talk, because without his eyewitness testimony, we have no case against James".

The investigation was far from over, but they were one step closer to the truth. The pieces of the puzzle were slowly falling into place, and Chief Swinson and Tisdale were determined to see it through to the end.

LIVING THAT LIFE

Chapter 58:

The Courtroom Drama

The courtroom was tense as James sat at the defendant's table, his eyes scanning the room with a cold, calculating gaze. Chief Swinson and Tisdale sat in the front row, their expressions stern and determined. They were here to catch James in a mistake, to prove that he was one of the shooters and planners of Tyrone's murder.

The prosecutor stood up, addressing the judge. "Your Honor, we have reason to believe that James was not only present at the scene of the crime but was also an active participant. We intend to prove that he played a crucial role in the planning and execution of Tyrone's murder."

James's lawyer, a sharp-dressed man with a confident demeanor, stood up to respond. "Your Honor, my client has been wrongfully accused. There is no concrete evidence linking him to the murder. The prosecution is relying on circumstantial evidence and hearsay."

LIVING THAT LIFE

Chapter 59:

The Threat

Meanwhile, the security guard who had shot James in the courthouse was living in fear. He had received a letter slipped under his door, a clear threat from James. It read, "You've already been warned about talking too much. Not only is your address and kids' school known but think you should know that your wife is wearing a lovely white dress. If you want her dress to stay white, keep your mouth shut, or she'll be wearing a white dress mixed with red. You decide!"

The security guard, trembling, handed the note to Chief Swinson. "He's threatening me, Chief. I was just doing my job. I acted in the line of duty."

Chief Swinson's expression softened. "We'll protect you, son. This note is the evidence we need to keep James behind bars. It shows his true colors."

Chapter 60:

The Trial Continues

Back in the courtroom, the prosecutor called the security guard to the stand. The guard, visibly shaken, recounted the events of that fateful day.

"I saw a man with a gun. I had no choice but to shoot. I was protecting myself and the others in the courthouse. It was my duty."

The prosecutor nodded, satisfied. "And what about this note and letter, officer? Did James threaten you?"

The guard handed the first note and the letter to the prosecutor, who then showed them to the judge. "Your Honor, this is clear evidence of James's intent to harm and intimidate. It shows his involvement in the murder and his willingness to go to any lengths to cover his tracks."

James's lawyer objected, why are you all saying James, when the officer said a man? He clearly didn't see who the man was. But the judge overruled him. "This note is admissible. It shows a clear pattern of behavior and intent."

LIVING THAT LIFE

Chapter 61:

The Verdict

After days of testimony and deliberation, the jury reached a verdict. James was found guilty of conspiracy to commit murder and intimidation by a witness and sentenced to only 6 months. However, due to the lack of concrete evidence linking him directly to the murder, he was not convicted of Tyrone's murder.

The security guard was cleared of all charges, the court ruling that he had acted in the line of duty. Chief Swinson and Tisdale, though satisfied with the outcome, knew that the truth about Tyrone's murder was still out there.

As they left the courtroom, Tisdale turned to Chief Swinson. "We did our best, Chief. But sometimes, the truth is harder to prove than we'd like."

Chief Swinson nodded, his eyes reflecting a mix of satisfaction and determination. "We'll keep digging, Tisdale. The truth always comes out in the end."

LIVING THAT LIFE

Chapter 62:

The Final Revelation

Chief Swinson asked Tisdale to take a ride with him. Once they made it to their destination, he saw that they were entering Lake Belton. Tisdale wants to ask a question, but he waits a little longer.

Chief Swinson and Tisdale stood by the lake, the water gently lapping at the shore. The sun was setting, casting a golden glow over the scene. Tisdale looked around, puzzled.

"Why are we out here in the middle of nowhere, Chief?" he asked, his voice tinged with curiosity and a hint of unease.

Chief Swinson smiled mysteriously and pointed over Tisdale's shoulder. "Because we have a guest," he said.

A low, calm voice came from behind Tisdale. "Tisdale, you miss me?"

Tisdale jumped, spinning around to see Tyrone standing there, a smirk on his face. "What? What is going on, Chief?" Tisdale exclaimed, his heart pounding.

Chief Swinson and Tyrone both laughed, the sound echoing across the lake. Tyrone extended his hand towards Tisdale. "Relax, Tisdale. I'm not a ghost. I'm very much alive."

Tisdale gathered himself, realizing what was happening. He reached out and shook Tyrone's hand. "You're alive? But how?"

Tyrone grinned. "Thanks to Chief Swinson here. He got a word from an informant about what was going to happen. He decided to put one of our police-issued bulletproof vests on me so it would look real. That's why I went straight down after I was shot."

Tisdale looked at Chief Swinson, his eyes wide with astonishment. "You knew about this the whole time?"

Chief Swinson nodded. "I had to keep it quiet, Tisdale. I wanted to be a couple of steps ahead. I didn't even involve you until now."

Tyrone's crew walked up, smirking at Tisdale. Tisdale looked around, still wary. "But what happened? How did you pull this off?"

Chief Swinson began to explain. "We needed to flush out the real culprits. By making it look like Tyrone was dead, we could draw out the people who were really behind the plot."

Tyrone spoke up, his voice firm. "It's good to know who your enemies are. Speaking of enemies, I have a few words for my so-called new leader, Mr. Darrell. Is he crazy? I'm hearing that he's letting this power that I allowed him to have go to his head. I never appointed him anyways. But I'll deal with him later."

Tyrone turned to Tisdale; his expression was serious. "And I got something for the Mathis family too. Yes, I have plans, especially for that little kid that shot me. Can you believe that? I got shot by a little boy; I can't let that go unreconciled." He and Chief Swinson exchanged a knowing glance.

Tyrone then looked at Tisdale, his tone turning stern. "By the way, you work for me now Tisdale."

Tisdale gave a stern frown towards Tyrone and then glanced over at Chief Swinson. All three of them exchanged serious, stern looks.

Tyrone continued, "I will continue to lay low for now, but I'll be back. I'm still sore from the gunshots. Even though I wore a police officer issued bullet proof vest, it still did a little damage. I'll be resting a while, but when it's time, you'll know." With that, he walked away, leaving Swinson and Tisdale staring at the water flowing up on the land.

As Tyrone disappeared into the distance, Tisdale turned to Chief Swinson. "What have we gotten ourselves into, Chief?"

Chief Swinson sighed; his gaze fixed on the horizon. "We did our job, Tisdale. We solved the case. But sometimes, the truth is more complicated than we thought."

Tisdale nodded; a sense of resolution settled over him. "Until next time, Chief."

Chief Swinson smiled, placing a hand on Tisdale's shoulder. "Until next time, Tisdale."

As they stood by the lake, the water flowing gently, they knew that their work was never truly done. But for now, they could rest, knowing that they had uncovered the truth and brought justice to those who needed it.

Chapter 63:

The After Plan

After taking a few weeks to gather his thoughts, Tisdale decided it was time to seek answers. He reached out to Pastor Glenn Williams, a man he had recently discovered was Chief Swinson's informant for the past twelve years. Tisdale had been surprised to learn that Glenn had managed to get off scot-free from his part in a house burglary he committed with Leroy and Marcus years ago.

Tisdale arranged to meet Glenn for lunch at The River Forest Smorgasbord restaurant in Belton, Texas. As he sat across from Glenn, Tisdale's mind was a whirlwind of questions and suspicions.

"Pastor Williams," Tisdale began, his voice steady but firm. "I know about your arrangement with Chief Swinson. I know you've been his informant for the past twelve years."

Glenn looked at Tisdale, his expression unreadable. "I see," he said, his voice calm. "And what do you plan to do with this information?"

Tisdale leaned in; his eyes locked onto Glenn's. "I want to know everything. I want to know why you've been working with Swinson, and I want to know what you know about the plans between him and Tyrone Turner."

Glenn sighed, his gaze drifting to the table. "Tisdale, It's complicated. I've been working with Swinson to keep the peace, to protect the community. But I've also been trying to keep an eye on Tyrone, to make sure he doesn't gain too much power."

Tisdale nodded, his mind racing. "I want to team up with you. I want to fight against whatever plans Swinson and Tyrone have. I want to bring them down and bring justice to this town."

Glenn looked up, his eyes meeting Tisdale's. "It won't be easy. Swinson and Tyrone are powerful, and they have a lot of people under their control. But if you're serious about this, I'm in."

Tisdale extended his hand across the table. "Then we have a deal, Pastor Williams. Together, we'll bring them down."

As they shook hands, Tisdale felt a sense of determination and purpose. He knew that the road ahead would be dangerous and uncertain, but he was ready to face whatever challenges lay ahead. With Glenn by his side, he was confident that they could uncover the truth and bring justice to Temple.

Chapter 64:

The New Alliance

Over the next few weeks, Tisdale and Glenn worked tirelessly to gather information and build a case against Chief Swinson and Tyrone Turner. They met in secret, sharing information and strategizing their next moves.

One evening, as they sat in Glenn's office, Tisdale laid out their plan. "We need to find concrete evidence linking Swinson and Tyrone to the murder of Tyrone's double. We need to prove that they staged the whole thing, and that Tyrone is still alive."

Glenn nodded, his expression serious. "I have a contact in the police department who might be able to help us. She has access to the evidence locker and might be able to get us the information we need."

Tisdale's eyes widened with excitement. "That's great, Glenn. We also need to find out what Swinson and Tyrone are planning next. We need to stay one step ahead of them."

Glenn agreed, and they spent the rest of the evening mapping out their strategy. They knew that the stakes were high, but they were determined to see it through to the end.

LIVING THAT LIFE

Chapter 65:

The Final Showdown

As Tisdale and Glenn continued their investigation, they uncovered a web of deceit and corruption that ran deep within the Temple community. They discovered that Chief Swinson and Tyrone Turner had been working together for years, using their power and influence to control the town and eliminate anyone who stood in their way.

One fateful night, Tisdale and Glenn found themselves face to face with Swinson and Tyrone in an abandoned warehouse on the outskirts of town. The tension was palpable as the four men stood in a tense standoff.

"Tisdale, Glenn," Swinson said, his voice cold and calculating. "I must say, I'm impressed. You've managed to uncover more than I thought you would."

Tyrone smirked, his eyes locked onto Tisdale. "But it ends here, Tisdale. You and Glenn are out of depth. You should have stayed out of this."

Tisdale stood his ground, his voice steady and firm. "We're not backing down, Swinson. We know the truth, and we're going to bring you and Tyrone down."

Glenn stepped forward; his expression resolute. "We have the evidence, Swinson. We know about the staged murder, and we know about your plans to take over the town. It's over."

Swinson's expression darkened, and he took a step towards Tisdale and Glenn. "You think you have all the answers, but you don't. You have no idea what you're up against."

As the tension reached its peak, a loud noise echoed through the warehouse, and a group of police officers burst through the doors. Tisdale and Glenn had anticipated the confrontation and had called for backup.

Swinson turned to Tyrone saying, "Tyrone run, go through that side door. Chief took out his gun and shot a couple of rounds the made enough distraction to allow enough time for them to escape. Tyrone yelled out, "Swinson come on!" Everything happened quickly, before Tisdale could get a clear view after Swinson shot, Swinson had disappeared with Tyrone. Glen managed to see Tyrone as he approached a vehicle that had pulled up and saw Chief Swinson running towards the same vehicle, but when Tisdale asked Glenn if he saw where they went, Glenn replied, "No, I couldn't see a thing after the shooting started, did you see anything Tisdale?" Tisdale said, "not a thing, man, I just knew we had them. What happened?"

The police were dispatched and began asking Tisdale questions about his falsifying a police raid. Tisdale didn't have an answer except, "I had them in sight until all of you come flying up in here with sirens blazing. If you would've did what I asked and come in as a raid, you know, never mind," and he walked off heading to his car but noticed that there was no sight of Glenn seen anywhere either.

Tisdale called Glen an hour later asking, "why did he leave?" Glen answered saying, "I apologize for leaving, but I am too deep into this police mess. One of the police officers that pulled up may have recognized me as an informant, that's why I backed out when they came forth, just in case he remembered me."

As Tisdale sat in his car listening to Glenn explain himself, he begins saying, "Glenn, I can't believe that you didn't see where Tyrone or Chief went". Glenn interrupts Tisdale saying, "I'm sorry Tisdale, but I did see where they went. They were both picked up by one of Tyrone's boys. It looked like Mike Whitherspoon, one of Wesley's partners. Tisdale asked, "Mike Whitherspoon? I thought he left town after Wesley got killed when Tyrone shot your niece. Well, James may have had something to do with that. That's why Swinson and Tyrone want him so badly. You see, this murder investigation that just turned into an attempted murder investigation isn't really about who shot Tyrone. Tisdale interrupts saying, "What? Why do you, a pastor, know more than me, the head officer on this case?" I understand your position in all of this. We'll keep on working together until we figure out how to get them both, but I sure do think that you know a lot more than you're saying. Speak up now. This is beginning to become more personal and important to me now. Glenn began explaining, "You see, Tyrone is after James for killing his brother Wesley on the day that he shot Leroy's daughter. Tisdale explained, you mean Tyrone's daughter. Glenn got quiet as Tisdale explained the situation concerning the Leroy, Tyrone and Terri saga.

LIVING THAT LIFE

Chapter 66:

A New Beginning

In the aftermath of the showdown, Tisdale and Glenn worked to rebuild the community and restore trust in the Temple Police Department. They knew that the road to recovery would be long and challenging, but they were determined to see it through.

As their conversation came to an end, Tisdale and Glenn knew that their journey was far from over. But they were ready to face whatever challenges lay ahead, knowing that they had the strength and determination to make a difference.

www.ingramcontent.com/pod-product-compliance
Lightning Source LLC
Chambersburg PA
CBHW020406150626
46554CB00012B/386